MANIFEST

DESTINY

The Path Towards Wisdom

DR. JAMERE BROWN SPENCER

Dedicated to:

Grandma Adelgunda Hidalgo Spencer

Grandma Pauline Coles

Grandma Evelyn May Grinnage

Grandpa Andrew Douglas Brown

Grandma Alma White

Grandma Mom & Pop Chavous

Grandpa John Llyod Spencer II

Mom Millie Collins

Randy Anderson Sr.

Aunt Alta Jones

Aunt Vincil Spencer

Aunt Mimi "Burnetha Lewis"

Pastor Temple

Aunt Shelia Carter

Jermaine "Tubby" Donnell

Manning Spencer

FOREWORD

Jamere has written a compelling book. He is from a far different background than me—African-American, the other side of the tracks, problems very different from mine—but he knows how to communicate. This book will make you think, push your limits, and give you the hope of a better spiritual life. I found a number of truths Jamere talks about to be very helpful in my own life, even as I edited the book. Rarely do I edit books that change my life, but this one did.

Jamere's concentration on the power of the Holy Spirit in a committed Christian's life was particularly searching and uplifting. His suggestion that most of us haven't tapped into all God has for us made me want what he spoke about.

His section on going into the closet that Jesus spoke of in the Sermon on the Mount (see the part on prayer in Matthew 6) really hit me hard. I never thought much about that passage before, but Jamere pulled out of that some amazing truths. Don't miss them. Those realities will change your prayer life and what it means to commune with the Lord of creation.

Next his thoughts on the three parts of the holy area of the Jewish Temple—the outer court, the Holy Place, and the Holy of Holies—is amazing. Jamere brought out things about these three parts of the Temple as three stages of a life committed to Christ. It thrilled me to read how an understanding of these would propel my life forward as a believer.

There are tough truths in this book, some you will never have heard before. Some will convict you deeply. And some will transform your life. The depth of Jamere Brown's understanding, though, will take you places never visited before and ultimately lived in. Read with an open, receiving mind. God will surely bless you.

Mark Littleton
Author of more than 100 Books
January 8, 2013

Acknowledgement

I would like to thank those who assisted me in developing this book. It's so many people to thank. First I would like to thank my beautiful girlfriend Sally for enabling me, encouraging me, and also assisting with editing this book. My son Joel for his patience, wisdom, and love.

Also all of my editors Mark Littleton, Rachel Starr Thomson, John L. Spencer III, Dick and Jeanie Moore, and Lyric Howard.

I would like to thank my Church Family, Pastors Alfonse Webb Jr. and Jennifer Webb, and the rest of the House of Refuge.

I would also like to thank my family. My Mother Sonja Brown and Father John Lloyd Spencer III. I would be nothing without their wisdom, knowledge and love. All of my talented brothers and sisters. Also my extended family my beautiful aunts, uncles, nieces, nephews and cousins. If I listed all of you by name it would take up another twenty pages. I have a big family. But from the oldest to the least you are all in my thoughts, even those who have gone before me. I can't forget about my LU(Lincoln University) Family also!

I would also like to thank Dr. Nick & Dr. Eva at Faith Bible College. I would like to thank, particular those who have influenced me spiritually. One of my Godmother's Rosa Drummond who is the Pastor of Redeemed Worship Center Located in Philadelphia, PA., Pastor Stan Archie and the rest of the Christian Fellowship staff. Pastor Ping Gonzales from Kansas City Restoration Church and Mrs. Elizabeth Briscoe Wilson from LU.

I would also like to thank my heavenly Father and my Lord and Savior Jesus Christ for given me this opportunity to present His word through me. I would also like to thank you the reader for sharing your time with me as we journey together. I don't claim to be perfect nor possess all understanding, but I will share with you my experiences.

Last and not least: I beg forgiveness of all those who have been with me over the course of the years and whose names I have failed to mention.

Copyright © 2013 by Jamere A. Brown Spencer

All rights reserved. This book or any portion thereof may not be reproduced or used in any manner whatsoever without the express written permission of the publisher except for the use of brief quotations in a book review.

Printed in the United States of America
First Printing, 2013
ISBN 978-0-9895299-1-4

All Scripture quotations marked "NIV" are taken from the Holy Bible, New International Version®. NIV®. Copyright © 1973, 1978, 1984 by International Bible Society. Used by permission of Zondervan. All rights reserved.

All Scripture quotations marked "KJV" are taken from the Holy Bible, King James Version. Public domain.

All Scripture quotations marked "NASB" are taken from the New American Standard Bible, © Copyright 1960, 1962, 1963, 1968, 1971, 1972, 1973, 1975, 1977, 1995 by The Lockman Foundation. Used by permission.

Scripture quotations marked "NLT" are taken from the Holy Bible, New Living Translation, copyright © 1996. Used by permission of Tyndale House Publishers, Inc., Wheaton, IL 60189 USA. All rights reserved.

Scripture quotations marked "DBY" are taken from The Holy Scriptures: A New Translation from the Original Languages by J. N. Darby. First published in 1890 by John Nelson Darby. Public domain.

Scripture quotations marked "NKJV" are taken from the New King James Version. Copyright © 1982 by Thomas Nelson, Inc.

Used by permission. All rights reserved.
Layout Design, Jamere A. Brown Spencer
Cover by Amygdala Design, amygdaladesign.net

Jamere A. Brown Spencer
P.O. Box 106015
Jefferson City, MO. 65109
www.jamere.org

Table of Contents

Introduction
Salvation in Knowing..8

Chapter 1
Knowing Wisdom 19

Chapter 2
Knowing the Word.. 37

Chapter 3
Knowing Love 57

Chapter 4
Knowing your Identity... 75

Chapter 5
Knowing your Father... 99

Chapter 6
Knowing the Secret Place 117

Chapter 7
Knowing Vision, Hope, & Faith 139

Chapter 8
Knowing to Wait.. 157

Chapter 9
Knowing Emptiness 173

Knowing Introduction

My heart admired what I saw as my eyes shifted from side to side. Another great wonder was on display—as grand as the others that had preceded it. Two gigantic hands had reached down from above to make a path, as solid as a mountain yet as aqueous as liquid. We all stood in the middle of a great sea, which now towered above us on each side. Instead of grabbing at our ankles, the muddy ground only propelled us forward. We were led by the man with the big stick—the stick he had used to swallow Pharaoh's snakes. The stick he now held across the waters.

The people of Israel looked to the leadership of Moses that day. His stick possessed no power, and neither did the one who wielded it.

A much more powerful force worked here. His purpose: to lead his chosen ones to salvation.

The chosen children of Israel were already God's. They were already saved through Abraham. Yet for a time before and during the exodus of Egypt, God provided what I like to call situational salvation. Situational salvation is when God moves through the very situation you are facing in this world, here and now. True eternal salvation is the greatest miracle of them all. However, our heavenly Father's desire is to bless you in a complete way—and that includes your life now, not just in a heavenly future.

When we explore the word *salvation*, we will discover its complex DNA. I often like to use the underlying Greek or Hebrew words to analyze the English translations of Scripture. To me, this is like a scientist who uses a microscope to zoom in closely.

Often when we study the Greek word, we will get a three-dimensional view, though the Spirit can also reveal this to us if we are receptive. In the New Testament, the Greek word for *salvation* or *saved* is *sozo*. A few examples are found in Scripture. The woman with the issue of blood said, "If I only touch his cloak, I will be healed [sozo]" (Matthew 9:21 NIV). Jesus said, "He who endures until

Knowing Introduction

the end shall be saved [sozo]" (Matthew 24:13 NLT). From the study of this word, you will see that it means spiritual or eternal salvation. It also means deliverance from bondage. When Jesus hung on the cross, those who watched told Jesus to save (sozo) himself (Matthew 27:40, 42 NIV). Paul looked at a crippled man who had faith to be saved (sozo).

All of us are in need of a situational salvation. It could be healing of the body, gaining employment, or a host of other situations. Often situational salvation will manifest in unexpected ways. Sometimes it manifests in ways we would not choose. God comes in ways we least expect, be it through a still, small voice or a babe in a manger. God manifests his presence in the most gritty and musty places. These places may be unknown, unfamiliar, and even uncomfortable. It's easy to shy away from the unknown, unfamiliar, and uncomfortable. However, if we do this, we could possibly miss our situational salvation!

I remember as a youth when we planned to move from Philadelphia to California, with a brief stop in Kansas City. Philly was all I knew. I enjoyed the block parties and hanging out with the other neighborhood kids. Most importantly, I knew I would miss all my Philly family. Going over to my godmommy Ethel's house on the weekend to play video games with my cousins, watching *Soul Train*, and playing with the dog meant a lot to me. Not to mention the cheese steaks and soft pretzels. As my mother made preparations for the move, I often asked why we had to leave.

She said it was for the best. My father encouraged us by singing the song "California, Here I Come." This song gave me visions of no winter and golden gates. For my parents, our move was about better employment opportunities and less violence. I had already been in a few fights. Drugs and gangs were all that appeared to await me if we stayed in Philadelphia. This journey was a situational salvation that had been provided for us. But a sad feeling still goes along with my memory of driving off for the last time. I

Knowing Introduction

remember looking at my cat, Toddy, who was forced to stay behind. Had it been my decision, I would have stayed with Toddy. Thankfully, the decision wasn't mine to make!

Throughout the Bible, there are stories of situational salvation. Often it comes in a strange guise. There was Naaman, commander of an army, who was a valiant leader (2 Kings 5). With the power of God, Naaman led King Aram to many situational salvations through battle. However, he had leprosy. Through a series of events, Naaman ended up traveling to the prophet Elisha's house. In moments he could be healed and able to continue his valiant work. But what happened next only angered Naaman.

Elisha didn't even have the courtesy to leave the house and greet his guest, who had traveled miles. Instead Elisha sent his servant, who directed Naaman to dip seven times in the muddy Jordan River. Naaman might have envisioned Elisha embracing him and inviting him into the house. Additionally, he may have daydreamed about how Elisha would lay hands on him to rid him of the leprosy. Here are his exact words: "I thought that he would surely come out to me and stand and call on the name of the Lord his God, wave his hand over the spot and cure me of my leprosy" (2 Kings 5:11 NIV). Nevertheless, Naaman reluctantly did as the prophet said and received his situational salvation.

Naaman received his healing (sozo), a miracle. I will share with you one important truth about miracles and salvation. The purpose of miracles is not only to demonstrate God's power to those who don't know him. *It's also to show his love and concern for those in hopeless situations.* Remember when Moses and the children of Israel were trapped by a great sea and a raging army? God did not provide a miracle to win the lost. He didn't provide a situational salvation so they could have an altar call for Pharaoh and his army. It was because the people needed deliverance. Don't believe God will only perform a miracle if someone comes to Christ! God is also concerned for the situational salvation of his children, including you.

Knowing Introduction

As you read this book, let it serve as your life jacket off a sinking ship. View this book as a boat escaping tyranny, searching for freedom across the great sea.

This book will take you down some very uncomfortable roads. It could cause you to feel spiritually dirty. But in what you may perceive as dirty and muddy water lies healing and the manifest presence of God. If there is some type of victory missing in your spiritual journey, then this book is for you. Often we lack victory because we have not experienced true discipleship in certain areas. In each chapter, we will creatively discuss basic discipleship principles. These principles will guide you to becoming a mature believer. You may not agree with everything I say. My hope is that you will discover what God desires for you to discover. More specifically, my hope is that you will experience the same victory the disciples experienced. I pray your journey leads you to your destiny.

Lessons from Turtle Island

Turtle Island appeared to be one of the most animated places in the world—like a precious living jewel designed by the Father. On this island, the leaves danced and waterfalls sang. Not only was it alive, but its beauty could be adored from shore to shore. Its majestic white-topped mountains stood tall and proud. The trees stretched to the heavens in esteem to God. Even the deserts brought forth life. The natives of the island said the land was, at one time, nothing but water. Then a giant tortoise arose from the water and offered its shell as land for the creatures. The people inhabiting the land cherished it. They poured themselves out for the land, and the land responded. This is how it was for years. Then, with sudden force, things began to change. A group of people sailed across the Sea of Blue Mystery and found Turtle Island. They too recognized the beauty of this bountiful land. Some of the people of Turtle Island welcomed them with open arms.

A few years later, more people began to sail across the great sea to the island. This group of people wanted dif-

Knowing Introduction

ferent results than the first group. They had a dream, a vision. Their dream was to control the entire island from one coast to the next. Many of those who had this dream would stop at nothing to see it come to past. As time progressed, their descendants attempted to bring forth a similar dream. They called this dream Manifest Destiny. Under the banner of Manifest Destiny, they believed God had ordained that they conquer and subdue Turtle Island. They pillaged the land and broke the natives. Turtle Island took a new form. No one referred to it as Turtle Island anymore; it was instead called *America*—more specifically, the United States of America. Many rejoiced in the change, but others were troubled.

What really struck some was the fact that the natives they fought would have freely shared their land. But the new Americans brought the wrong mentality. Their belief that the natives of Turtle Island were savages gave them a sense of superiority. Their superiority produced a sense of entitlement to the land and animosity toward the natives. The wrong path was chosen, leading many down a road of pain and destruction that could have been avoided. Much of the conflict centered on treasures the newcomers already possessed. Yes, conflicts were inevitable, but many were unnecessary. Instead of coming in friendship as they could have done, the conquerors employed trickery and deceit to strong-arm the island away from the natives.

It's here that we move away from the story of the United States and its conquest to the life of the believer in Christ.

First, a Lesson

We can all learn a valuable lesson from Turtle Island. As believers, we too believe God has given us access to precious jewels—a Manifest Destiny of sorts. However, like those who traveled the mysterious blue sea to find new lands and places to settle, we often use false methods to obtain what is already rightfully ours. When we use our own methods to take from and win over those we regard as adversaries, we come up short. When we come

Knowing Introduction

up short, we fail to possess the full blessing.

The Hebrews fell into the same trap. God told Abraham to walk the length and breadth of the land, and he would give him all of it (Genesis 13:17). This involved a large portion of land. It stretched south and north from the Nile River in Egypt to Lebanon. West to east, it ran from the Mediterranean Sea to the Euphrates River (Genesis 15:18, Joshua 1:4). However, as history has revealed, Abraham's descendants only possessed a small portion of this land. They failed to listen to the wisdom that God freely offered.

The Devil Got Involved Too

The Deceiver played a prominent role in the grand theft of the inheritance of God's chosen people. He led them into all kinds of foolish and evil behavior, such as the ten spies who rejected the idea of conquering the land the first time because of fear (Numbers 14) and the forfeiture of the northern kingdom of Israel because of rank, arrogance, and stubbornness (1 Kings 11).

Many of us can relate to the experience of someone stealing from us. I have had many things taken from me. One of the most visible was my ten-foot basketball goal with NBA regulation basketball nets, located in our paved backyard. This was a gift given to me by my father for graduating from the sixth grade. Not many people could afford such things in our neighborhood. My father worked very hard to provide it for me. Early one Saturday morning, my brother-in-law brought over my nephew. He knocked on the door, and I answered. Before I could say, "Come in," he asked me where we had placed my basketball goal. I thought he was joking. "It's where it has been the last two months."

"Maybe it fell down," he answered, "because I didn't see it when we drove past your driveway." I hurried to the side yard, and there was the big gaping hole where my basketball goal had once stood. It was gone. I couldn't believe someone would take it. The most precious gift I'd ever received had been stolen!

Knowing Introduction

Memories of how we had originally put it there flashed through my head. My father, my brothers, and I had cleaned an area full of rocks, glass, and other debris. We spray-painted a free-throw line on the concrete. Then we each painted our names on the wall around it. I had placed all the rocks I could find over the sandbags and iron rods used to secure the goal in the ground.

With it missing, my father and I drove around the neighborhood to find it. We spotted no traces of it. About two weeks later, my brother-in-law discovered it about five blocks away in someone else's driveway. We drove past the house with him to confirm it. It was my basketball goal indeed. However, the thieves had tried to change it. They had spray-painted it, attempting to deceive us.

That basketball goal brought much pleasure not only to me but also to the other children in the neighborhood. As a young man, I hoped to make it to the NBA someday. My brothers, my friends, and I spent countless hours winning imaginary championships. Thieves took the basketball goal away and repainted it to deceive anyone who might come around searching for it.

Something that belonged to me was no longer mine. But how could we prove it?

The Demonic Realm

This is how the demonic realm operates. They utilize many of their tools—deception, lying, temptation, coaxing, pushing, ridiculing, outright theft—to steal from you. Demonic entities have used such trickery to rob the church of many precious jewels. Some of the bounty they have taken and redesigned, making it look like it never belonged to the church. They have been so clever in this deception that those from whom they took were deceived. Some of the victims of this deception believe a robbery never occurred. They say these jewels have just faded and are no longer required.

Many years have now passed since we lost these great treasures. What are these treasures, you may ask? Here I

Knowing Introduction

am speaking of the spiritual gifts. These gifts are listed in 1 Corinthians 12:7–11. Though their existence and power are still recorded in the text of Scripture, we have lost the wisdom to manifest and operate in them.

In the early years of the church, many gave their lives as martyrs. These events occurred centuries after the apostolic age, meaning nearly two hundred years had passed since the twelve apostles walked the earth. Yet there were still believers being martyred. Not because they were eyewitnesses of the resurrection. So what did these martyrs experience that was worth dying for? What was the quality of their lives? Irenaeus, one of the early church fathers, speaks of this in a text titled *Against Heresies*. In book II, chapter 32, he writes of laymen who had visions, prophesied, healed the sick, and raised the dead. This was in the second century. Another example is St. Hilary of Poitiers. St. Hilary, as discovered in some of his writings, came to expect the manifestation of the charismatic gifts. This was occurring in the fourth century. Still another of the church fathers, Origen, noted that believers possessed the ability to cast out demons. There is no doubt that the gifts of the Holy Spirit were still prominent in the early church.

Besides the spiritual gifts, other extraordinary experiences happened in the early days of the church that mainstream Christianity today is lacking. The Bible records many of them.

What are these extraordinary experiences? How about walking on water or disappearing in the midst of the crowd (John 5:13, Matthew 14:22)? What about the time and space travel that the apostle John experienced (Revelation 4)? Often, on certain Christian television stations, you will hear people proclaim such testimonies. In particular one of my favorite programs is *Sid Roth, It's Supernatural*. These stories sound outlandish or even heretical.

Knowing Introduction

> Heal the Sick   WALK ON WATER
> You are more than ordinary   Open Eye & Ears
> **MIRACLES**   DREAMS & VISIONS
> You are Extraordinary
> RAISE THE DEAD   *Time & Space Travel*

However, is it possible these people are simply partaking of what is to come (Hebrews 6:5)? What I'm asking you to do is not to accept these events as doctrine but to consider the possibilities.

Just for a moment, examine this question with your heart. Is it possible God is calling us to walk in this supernatural manner? To execute these great exploits? Or have I, and so many others, watched too many science fiction movies? Yes to great exploits; no to movies!

In my own life I have had angels manifest, providing direction; I have seen raging animals halted by the name of Jesus. With God, the extraordinary is still a part of our world.

Nevertheless, time passed, and so did this supernatural side to the believer's faith. The wisdom to operate in these stolen gifts and dimensions is all but gone. They are myths, legends, and fables in today's society. How could something so powerful slip through the cracks? What happened? Why were they lost? Sometimes things become lost because we have misplaced them. In this case, to some degree, we have actually silenced these gifts.

There is an interesting prophecy in Zechariah 6:8 concerning this topic: "Then he called to me, 'Look, those going toward the North Country have given my Spirit rest in the land of the north'" (NIV).

Let's examine the words rest and north in this prophecy. The original Hebrew word for rest is *nuwach*. This means to put to rest, to leave, or even to silence. So this Scripture can be interpreted to say that in the North Country, the Spirit has been silenced. We all understand the globe is divided into two hemispheres, Northern and Southern. If you were to analyze the testimonies of miraculous

Knowing Introduction

much greater in the Southern Hemisphere. Could this be a coincidence, or did God foreknow that his church would treat the gifts of his Spirit this way? Is it possible that those from the more prosperous nations of the north have silenced the Spirit of God? I believe this is one of the reasons we have lost such gifts. Other times, they have become lost because someone has stolen them. However, in both instances, a familiar foe lurks in the shadows.

This foe, a mysterious, dark figure, has subtly hidden these treasures by convincing believers to forgo them. It seemed at first to be a reasonable exchange. With the compiling of manuscripts, the church now had the Bible. We had something tangible. Academic, sound doctrine crept in, and we exchanged it for the intangible. A personal experience with the Holy Spirit only confirms the written Word. Nevertheless, truth was bartered for half-truths. With each passing day, a portion of the truth was relinquished. The church was bamboozled. They already possessed sound doctrine, but they needlessly exchanged the gifts of the Spirit for what they perceived to be a more solid reality. The manifestation of gifts and the Word are meant to operate hand in hand. We already possessed both, so why did we feel the need to give one up for the other?

This dark figure executed a similar coup centuries before. As history recalls, it was a day that changed all other days.

Beginning of Darkness

It had to be one of the darkest days known to man, though it didn't begin that way. Like every other day in paradise, the love of the Father radiated throughout the garden. The beautiful flowers rocked back and forth with the wind. The rocks praised God.

The mosquito, whose thirst was not for blood, flew around in the delight of glorifying God. The animals danced along the pasture, living in fear and reverence for God and at peace with man. But as the day passed, a strange eeriness began to slither across paradise. The eeriness manifested itself in the form of a serpent. He engaged a woman and enticed her into a deadly exchange. He said that if she partook of a particular tree, she would be like God. She would change her current state for a godly state.

If Eve had only understood that what she was being offered, she already possessed! The serpent said she would be like God (Genesis 3:4). However, in a sense, she was already like God in ways she was ignorant of (Genesis 1:26). You know the story of Eve's temptation as well as I do: she ate the fruit in disobedience to God, and Adam followed suit. As a result of man's yielding to the serpent, the Devil became the master of men (Romans 6:16). Paradise was lost and soon became only a legend to some. A world once full of life and hope became a place of deception and darkness. This darkness crept across the universe, even into galaxies yet to be discovered.

However, a new dawn approaches us now. A new day overshadows the former darkness. As this new day comes upon us, it is our duty to discover our weapons and unmask the Enemy. His day grows short because the kingdom is at hand (Revelation 12:12, Matthew 3:2). Our destiny will no longer be denied.

Destiny

Like the natives and pilgrims of Turtle Island and the Hebrews who left Egypt, we too have a destiny that God desires to manifest in our lives. However, we must prepare ourselves to receive his divine wisdom. We must reclaim what God has offered us from the beginning. Some of the wisdom we need can be found in the pages of this book. However, much more wisdom is unprintable and can only been seen through the eyes of the heart. Scripture assures you that you have the mind of Christ (1 Corinthians 2:16). My hope is that this book will enable you to access the wisdom God has placed within you as we take this journey together.

CHAPTER 1
KNOWING WISDOM

Chapter 1: Knowing Wisdom

A month had passed as I walked the path. Only a few more steps, and my journey would be complete. I would be free. My mentors were correct when they said the path of the dead trees led to life. As I approached my destination, I felt like someone had raised me from the dead. It felt as if heaven were stretching out her arms, beckoning me to walk faster. Since childhood, I had dreamed of finding such a place. My ancestors had passed down stories from generation to generation of what it was once like—to be free. No, it was no paradise, but it was our life. The land was grand, and love abounded. All was not perfect, however; corruption brewed from within. My ancestors were betrayed from within and given into bondage. They were forced to sail past the end of the earth as they understood it—out of freedom and into slavery.

Their stories motivated me to leave the living hell of bondage. Since my birth, slavery was all my spirit and body had known. The physical pain that radiated from the gashes on my back was nothing in comparison to the spiritual pain we all felt. We received treatment not even an animal was worthy of. Our equals demeaned us in many ways; we were even given names unknown to our heritage. Theirs was a daily attempt to assassinate our spirits and will to live. However, our spirits yearned to break free.

A man once put in writing what I truly desired. In this document, he wrote, "We hold these truths to be self-evident, that all men are created equal, that they are endowed by their Creator with certain unalienable Rights, that among these are Life, Liberty and the pursuit of Happiness." The purpose of my journey was not only for me but also for the generations that would follow. Life, liberty, and the pursuit of happiness would only happen if I took action. But it would take more than my own will to complete this journey. It would take the effort of an organized community.

Thank God such a community existed. They orchestrated a plan only God could have composed. Little did I know these mundane objects would lead me to freedom. The quilt, the lawn jockey, and the conductor all guided me down this

Chapter 1: Knowing Wisdom

concealed road to a place I like to call heaven. My mind reminisced as my feet finally crossed the border. My journey down this hidden road, or as we called it, the Underground Railroad, had guided me to Canada but more specifically to the gift of freedom.

Historians write that more than one hundred thousand slaves traveled the Underground Railroad to freedom. Assistance from Native Americans, African Americans, and Caucasian Americans sped them along. Surely there is not a single person on earth who does not desire freedom. But what if you did not know you were in bondage? Would you desire freedom? Would you dream of more?

Many of us have dreams of a better life. We long to open up foster homes for children. We imagine a world without wars. We look ahead and hope our children will have better lives than we do. And some look at the horizon and wonder if they will ever one day have enough to eat, a shelter to live in, and a family to cling to. We all have dreams. However, we often throw away those dreams because we see them as nothing more than mere wishes, wisps in the wind. As a result, we remain bound to the elements that hold our dreams captive.

There are many truths to be learned about your dreams. This truth frees us from bondage as we begin our journey. Like Jesus says, "Then you will know the truth, and the truth will set you free" (John 8:32 NIV). Many truths can bring you out of bondage and cause your dreams to become manifest. What are these truths that lead to freedom, and how can we discover them?

Discovery

I like to compare these truths to a treasure. This treasure is not silver, gold, or precious jewels; this treasure is wisdom. Wisdom frees us from the bondage of the world. If you are interested in this freedom, then, like our friends on the Underground Railroad, you must go down a hidden and concealed path to find it.

Chapter 1: Knowing Wisdom

Concealed Wisdom

God is the arbiter of concealing and revealing. Job says that wisdom is hidden from the eyes of every living thing (Job 28:20–21). But why is something so beneficial so hidden? Why would God conceal the very thing he desires us to possess? Is God holding back?

The trail of the Underground Railroad provides us with revelation for this question. If you traveled down the Underground Railroad, many symbols guided your way—but only if you looked. In a sense, they were hidden in plain sight. The purpose was to conceal those symbols from some and reveal them to others. For instance, quilts of different colors, markings, and patterns hung over fences. Triangles on those quilts meant that prayer was available. Wagon wheels instructed you to pack your bags, because you were about to go on a long journey. Symbols of direction were all around. Helpers draped them over fences so it appeared as if the quilts were drying. In reality, they offered wisdom for the journey ahead.

Similarly, God conceals his wisdom from some and reveals it to others. Proverbs 25:2 says, "It is the glory of God to conceal a matter; to search out a matter is the glory of kings" (NIV). For a long time, I pondered this Scripture. It seemed like a riddle. Why was God hiding valuable treasure from us? Why does he make us search? Why does concealing a truth bring glory to God? The answer to this riddle can be found in the heart of the abolitionist.

Abolitionism

In the days of the Underground Railroad, men and women of all ethnic backgrounds placed hidden symbols in everyday objects. They concealed these markings to change the destiny of many. Once one slave became free as he learned and followed the symbols, how do you think the designer of the quilt felt? What about the person who intentionally placed the lawn jockey in his front yard, indi-

Chapter 1: Knowing Wisdom

cating safe passage to the slave? As the free slave revealed these things to his bound friends, they too took the path and escaped, fulfilling the hearts of the people who had left the symbols and providing them with the joy of giving and helping. Knowing they had played a key role in the freedom of a human being brought them joy and glory. Not glory for the mere sake of being honored or praised but the glory of having accomplished something great.

They didn't care about being mentioned in history books; their only motivation was freedom for others who dreamed of it.

In this way, the abolitionists were similar to God. When we find freedom, it brings him glory. This is not only true of eternal salvation, but of so much more. The key to our journey is to understand the symbols that surround us. The quilts on the Underground Railroad sent a message loud and clear but only to the discerning eye. I suspect that for some slaves these images meant nothing, and they never found true freedom. They were doomed to remain in bondage. But to those who possessed this knowledge, it provided deliverance from bondage.

Bound

This is one reason many of us remain in bondage. We do not discern in our minds and hearts the symbols of wisdom. Wisdom stretches out its hand, pleading that someone take hold of it, yet it goes unnoticed (Proverbs 1:20–24). Why do we have difficulty noticing wisdom? After all, who wants to behave foolishly? I believe we don't notice wisdom because we don't know what it looks like. When we are in a state of ignorance, we may not see what is right in front of us.

A recent example happened at the grocery store. My wife sent me to purchase a few remaining ingredients for tuna salad: celery, relish, mayonnaise, and tuna. I took on this task confidently. When I reached the store, I quickly filled my basket with the first three items. When I came down to the last ingredient, I was at a loss.

Chapter 1: Knowing Wisdom

I searched all of the logical places: the frozen fish section, the canned meat area, and even the ice cream aisle. With no luck, I paced back and forth. I refused to ask for directions because I knew I would find it eventually! Thirty minutes later, I was left with no choice. In confusion and defeat, I called my wife, explaining my problem. Like a GPS navigator, she guided me over the phone back to the canned meat aisle. In my ignorance, I still didn't see it, but if the tuna had eyes, it would have clearly seen me! Still on the phone with my wife, I said, "The only thing I see in this area is something called Chicken of the Sea." She laughed because that was exactly what I needed. I was unable to recognize it because of my lack of familiarity with the product. My mind was set on something else, causing an inability to see the solution.

This is how wisdom is. Often it stands right in front of us and even within us. In ignorance, we ignore it, trample it, and sometimes even rebuke it. Meanwhile, we look for wisdom in foolish things like fortune cookies, talk shows, and sometimes even friends. But we should only look to those as confirmations of wisdom, if even that is what they are.

Real Wisdom

What does real wisdom look like? How do we discern it from foolishness or ignorance? We face daily decisions that require wisdom. Imagine spotting a stranger in need of a ride on a rainy day. He could be a killer, a robber, or an escaped convict, or maybe he is indeed just someone who needs a ride. Which is the right choice? Can knowing wisdom be as simple as solving the algebra formula $x + 9 = 18 - 2x$? We know by calculation that $x = 3$ in the previous problem. But what about x when it comes to wisdom for believers? Our x can be found in James 3:17: "But the wisdom that comes from heaven is first of all pure; then peace-loving, considerate, submissive, full of mercy and good fruit, impartial and sincere."

When you pass the guy walking down the street, you

Chapter 1: Knowing Wisdom

need to apply James 3:17 first. Is the action you're taking peace-loving; is it sincere, impartial, considerate? This is what wisdom looks like in every situation. If the action itself is fine, what about the motive of this individual? How can I use wisdom to discern his motive? Perhaps we can learn from one of the most perplexing stories of the Bible on discernment.

This is recorded in 1 Kings 13. The Lord gave his prophet specific directions not to eat or drink but to go directly home. As the younger prophet followed the Lord's direction, he encountered an older prophet of the Lord. This prophet insisted that the younger prophet go with him to eat and drink. The younger prophet detoured from his path, ultimately causing his sudden death.

I'm sure the younger prophet believed that his x in this situation was a right choice.

Nevertheless, we are now presented with an opportunity to learn from his deadly mistake.

The correct answer in this case was for him to stay on course and not be distracted. In life, we will encounter situations where the other person's motive is not revealed, and we cannot know whether good consequences will follow our good intentions. This is where we must base our decision on the word God gives directly through his written Word or Spirit. I have seen many strangers in need of a ride, some even giving an indication with their thumb. I have driven past many of these people, often wondering if I should take a risk. Once I saw a younger guy walking down the street with no shoes on. It was raining. *Should I offer him a ride?* I wondered. Earlier that day I had actually studied the parable of the good Samaritan. Often God will test us on what we have read to see if we will apply it. This younger man was someone I probably would have passed up based on his appearance. But when I saw him, my mind was drawn to the parable. The Spirit was confirming the right action in my heart.

Determining the x in our lives through the written Word of God can be a difficult task. As a matter of fact, it

Chapter 1: Knowing Wisdom

can be a nearly impossible task without the Holy Spirit. We deal with situations that have never been recorded in the text. There are diseases people have been diagnosed with that were never recorded in Scripture. We face situations daily that can't be solved by using the Bible as if it were a twelve-step program. This is when many believers end up on a dead-end road. Their perception is that there is no way out, no answer to be found. Some decide to take alternate routes, leading to deception and false spiritual practices. However, their answer is indeed in there. We must learn to apply the truths from the Word with the leading of the Holy Spirit. This will result in finding the solution for x.

$$X=?$$

Wisdom may lead us down paths we don't expect. I once found myself on a road I didn't know existed. On this path, I discovered teachings I never thought could have been written in the Bible.

Many of these truths have been forsaken by both Western and Eastern Christianity. At times I felt I must have gotten off track. I second-guessed what I now understand to have been the leading of the Holy Spirit. As I investigated the Word, I became surrounded by what I viewed as mystical teachings. But they were all confirmed by the Bible! The Scriptures are full of mystical elements, including talking animals, people walking through walls, dinosaurs, invisible beings, and inanimate objects that groan and cry. The Word is comparable to one of those high-budget animated children's movies. Freedictionary.com defines *mysticism* as "not apparent to intelligence or the senses." This definition seems to align with 1 Corinthians 2:7–8: "No, we declare God's wisdom, a mystery that has been hidden and that God destined for our glory before time began. None of the rulers of this age understood it, for if they had, they would not have crucified the Lord of glory" (NIV). Could it be that the Word we cherish

Chapter 1: Knowing Wisdom

contains elements of *mysticism*? What if it does, despite what you believe? What will your response be?

Most of us get stuck on the word *mysticism*, but its meaning is similar to the word *mystery*. Job was unable to fathom the mysteries of God (Job 11:7). But years later, Paul would tap into a few of these mysteries in 1 Corinthians 4:1: "This, then, is how you ought to regard us: as servants of Christ and as those entrusted with the mysteries God has revealed" (NIV).

How about you? If presented with something contrary to what you believe and understand that turns out to be actual truth, how would you respond?

In the year 1633, an older scientist named Galileo taught what the church believed to be heresies. He taught his followers that the earth revolved around the sun, according to the theories of Copernicus. In fear of being burned at the stake like his predecessor, Giordano Bruno, a generation earlier, Galileo recanted his statement. He spent the last seven years of his life on house arrest with no visitors allowed. Just think of the knowledge and wisdom forced to waste away in a hidden room. Yes they apologized, but the damage was done. Since that time many others with spiritual wisdom and knowledge have faced the same fate as Galileo. Because, we were not ready to receive such treasures. However, let's not tread the same path those before us have taken! I once heard a great teacher on eschatology say the most humbling statement. He said his belief is that the church will not be raptured until after the great tribulation. However, he also said that if the rapture does occur before that, he will not hold on to a tree, saying, "God, you're not supposed to come yet." In the matters before you, will you continue to hold on to your own personal understanding, or will you let go and let God? Will you peruse these mysteries like a king who searches out a matter? Like a slave who searches for freedom? Or will you be like those who see and never perceive, and hear but never understand, as Jesus said some would be in Mark 4:12?

Chapter 1: Knowing Wisdom

Here is a warning to the reader: you must be prepared to take this journey. As we travel further down the path, you will be challenged as you attempt to discern light from darkness. The path to wisdom is like walking down a trail with only a lamp to guide you. You can only see a few feet in front of you, and everything else is darkness (Psalm 119:105). Thus, to gain real wisdom and to go far down this spiritual journey, you must have discernment. We will encounter situations in which it will be difficult to determine where the darkness ends and the light begins, especially when it appears that they are merging. Wisdom is as vivid and diverse as the colors of the rainbow.

Not even my words can conjure up a definition to describe how beautiful wisdom is. But if I could, I would say it blends in like a scenic view of the purple evening sky, unifying the orange rays that radiate from the sun. When looking at such an image, it's difficult to discern where one color ends and the other begins. Only one who is determined and focused will have the ability to determine the borders of each color. That is how a good artist mirrors what he sees through a painting. He learns to differentiate the variation of colors through determination and focus. This is how we must learn to discern wisdom from foolishness or ignorance.

Such discernment becomes complex, because sometimes darkness appears as light. Like the Bible says, Satan can appear as an angel of light (2 Corinthians 11:14). It becomes even more perplexing when what you believe is darkness turns out to actually be light. That is what the disciples experienced on the sea when they saw a "ghost" who was actually Jesus (Matthew 14:26). In order to know the difference, we must become wise.

I believe the church has unintentionally chased away the wisdom God has to offer because they denounced it as something else or simply ignored it as foolishness. But often wisdom is couched in terms that seem so simple that many people dismiss it.

Chapter 1: Knowing Wisdom

We can learn spiritual discernment by applying principles we have learned from our own lives. If we take time to notice, we will see that each day, the world teaches us a new lesson. Just like Jesus used everyday parables to teach spiritual truths, we can use our life experience as personal parables.

Lessons from the Streets

Growing up in the rough parts of the inner city was always a challenge for me, as it is for many. Many entered a life of crime because that was all they saw ahead. As a result, they ended up serving a sentence in prison. Often they were killed before their time. There is no pleasure in knowing neighborhood kids who have fallen victim to drugs, poverty, or even worse. Many of these souls had potential to be great doctors, scientists, and teachers.

With prayer and the protection of the Holy Spirit, I avoided many of the traps my peers succumbed to. However, I have to credit something else for my success: street smarts. I developed much worldly wisdom from my dealings growing up in a low-income area. When you witness drug deals from your bedroom window and friends drugged out on the street, it changes you mentally. Gunshots and police sirens were as common as the wind blowing.

Living in an inner-city community exposes one to many dangers. To the ignorant, it could result in death or a beat down. I learned to avoid wearing too much of certain colors in order to avoid gang affiliation. In some areas, I even had to monitor the direction my ball cap faced. Even looking at someone in what they deemed "the wrong way" could lead to danger. In time I learned to avoid certain streets, use alternate routes, and most importantly, not do anything stupid. One false move could place me in serious trouble.

One time, accidentally cutting someone off almost got me into severe danger. I was driving with a broken mirror and never saw the other car. Suddenly, I found myself

Chapter 1: Knowing Wisdom

blocked in as they pulled up to the driver's side of my car. I had nowhere to go. The three men from the other vehicle had bloodshot eyes and a spirit of death with them. Fear very nearly consumed me as the guy in the back reached under his seat for something. I knew only a few items that would be stored there. Suddenly, my street smarts kicked in. As the Spirit led me, I talked myself out the situation. If I had made one more mistake, I probably wouldn't be writing about this today.

Possessing street smarts is even more needed in the spiritual world. If you're lacking in this area, you place yourself in a position of certain death. God desires that we have spiritual street smarts, but he gives them a different name. He says to be "wise as serpents" (Matthew 10:16 NIV). But what does that mean exactly? How is a serpent wise? Usually when we think of serpents, we consider deception, venom, hissing. Ever since Eden, we have associated the serpent with the curse, the Devil, and pure evil. But this is not a comprehensive view of the serpent. God created all creatures, including the serpent (Genesis 1:25). In that same breath there is something very wicked about the symbol of the serpent. However, there is a characteristic of the serpent that Jesus desires us to possess.

All animals symbolize an attribute of God. We often associate Jesus with the lion, since Scripture refers to him as the Lion of Judah (Revelation 5:5). But Satan is also referred to as a roaring lion (1 Peter 5:8). Likewise, the serpent is often identified with deception, but it was also an image of healing (Numbers 21:8–9), and Jesus associated it with wisdom. This wisdom is not sneaky or deceptive, but discerning and calculating. In ancient culture the serpent also represented a symbol of wisdom, perhaps because of its ninja-like behavior.

Freedictionary.com defines *ninja* as "Japanese mercenary agents who were trained in the martial arts and hired for covert operations such as assassination and sabotage." At my job, my coworkers refer to me as a ninja.

Chapter 1: Knowing Wisdom

After reading that definition, it seems like a ninja could be a bad, deceptive, and ruthless person. But the reason my coworkers endowed me with the title is because of my behavior at work (and no, I'm not trying to assassinate or sabotage anyone). In their eyes, I appear covert. I'm often able to slip through the exit door unnoticed, even though my coworkers' desks are positioned with a clear view to the exit. Time and time again they will call my name, and when they don't hear my response, they will look into the office.

They'll say, "The ninja is at it again!" It makes me laugh. They once told my wife that I'm a ninja because "he is very *sneaky*." Of course, the word sneaky has a negative connotation with it. My wife immediately responded by saying, "He is not sneaky." Then she began to think of her experience with me and how I have always surprised her with different gifts. I have managed to sneak several household items into the house without her knowing. She then responded, "He is sneaking. But sneaking in a good, ninja-like way." Much like a ninja, a serpent becomes invisible by camouflaging its appearance to its surroundings. In preparation for an attack, serpents survey their environment. Every move they make is tactical. Then, when the timing is right, they capture their surprised prey. They complete their assignment.

This is how God desires for us to respond in every situation. We are to operate like a ninja or serpent to accomplish the purpose of God. Our preparation comes through prayer, fasting, worshiping, and studying the written Word. This allows us to become one with the Father. In our case, we are not capturing surprised prey but freeing slaves who are bound by the deception of the enemy and our comrades who are held hostage. In some cases this involves winning the lost, and in other cases it means bringing a situational salvation. This is where the second part of Jesus' saying comes in: he said to "be as harmless as doves" (Matthew 10:16 NIV). The dove represents the Holy Spirit, who can only operate through love. We are

Chapter 1: Knowing Wisdom

to be wise and calculating as we operate in love.

Possessing this type of wisdom will help you mature in your spiritual growth. Wisdom will give you strength. I once had a friend who considered himself a druid. He was very vocal about the sorcery and other practices he participated in. He had some very interesting information, and he even made attempts to make me his apprentice. I made him aware I was a follower of Christ, though I was interested in what he had to say. On one occasion a young believer was listening to our conversation. My friend struck fear in her by saying, "Tonight when I go home, I will meditate and come into your bedroom" as he laughed wickedly. She immediately started to cry. I told him, "There is no need for you to do this." I also told the girl, "There is no need to fearful if you believe in God."

If you allow wisdom to operate, you will grow comfortable and confident in what you believe and will not be easily led astray. I'm able to read any spiritual book and listen to people of different religions and not lose who I am or what I believe. In some cases, what I read and what I hear only confirms what the written Word has already revealed to me. I have a friend who is Muslim, and he speaks of his dedication to prayer, and this only motivates me to share my prayer life and pray more. Often in life, many issues are not black and white but a lot of gray. But within those gray areas, if you apply wisdom, you can determine the black and white.

As street-smart, calculating believers, we must move away from a cookie-cutter Christianity. Life happens with layers of meaning, and God wants us aware of this. He is transcendent, so he can be symbolized by a wise serpent, a conquering lion, or even a helpless lamb. Yet those symbols can also become corrupted, given their alternative meanings. I had a friend who wouldn't allow any stuffed owls in her house because of her spiritual understanding of owls. She was told that witches used owls as gateways to spy on people. However, owls are the workmanship of God (Psalm 8:8).

Chapter 1: Knowing Wisdom

In the same way, we need to dig deep into our faith and see the layers of meaning and possibility in God.

Psalm 12:6 says Scripture is refined several times, meaning there can be several revelations in one verse. Though not every verse will fall into this pattern, for many there is a historical, literary, allegorical, narrative, life application, and prophetic interpretation all in one verse. One example is the church of Philadelphia in Revelation 3. During the lifetime of the apostle John, there actually was a local church in the Greek city of Philadelphia to whom this letter was written. However, it has also been said that this church represents a particular church age.

It also has a personal revelation that we can apply in our own lives. In a sense, viewing the Word this way may seem to bring disorder and confusion. This is no doubt a real risk, especially with the spiritually immature. Many false prophets have misinterpreted Scripture and produced ungodly teachings—women who are forbidden to teach, men who can't marry, men who can have multiple wives, and a host of other errors. So how do we set the rules to bring order and prevent error? This is no new question. Since the beginning of church history, there have been attempts to address such issues.

The Councils of Nicea, Trent, and Constantinople were such attempts. Battles raged, resulting in doctrine and interpretations we hold dear today. Yet a portion of what God desired to execute through those early believers remains incomplete in various spheres of Christianity. This is because, on some issues, they were unwilling to follow the leading of the Spirit.

Though it was not their intent, they placed God in a box. They limited the move of the Spirit with their interpretation of Scripture. To them it was the right choice; after all, there was a lot of heretical teaching going on. This human effort to identify and interpret Scripture with a little help from the Spirit resulted in a lot of relevant and key selections of Scripture and doctrine. The main problem was the emphasis on a human effort to unify

Chapter 1: Knowing Wisdom

the church instead of letting the Spirit have full rein. The church created a dependency on man and took power away from the laymen. They allowed their own thoughts to dominate their interpretation of the written Word. However, a new day awaits us!

This day is not a day of new revelation but of full revelation. If our response is like that of our forefathers' response, we will never mature. We must take risks where our forefathers came up short. The risk is simply allowing the Spirit to lead us—even if that involves relinquishing centuries of what we once interpreted as truth. We are to discern God's Word correctly with the leading of his Spirit.

The Spirit of discernment will provide wisdom for everything you face. It causes you to be wise like the serpent and even wiser. We can only abide in this wisdom when we draw near to God (James 4:8). This doesn't mean increasing your church attendance or sitting closer to the pulpit. It's so much more. It can be compared to going to Disney World. If you only walk through the gates and sit down near the entrance for a couple hours and then leave, you have not experienced Disney World to its fullest. If you venture deeper into the park and ride the rides, eat the cuisine, and watch the shows, you will have a completely different experience. Yet even in all of that, you have not truly experienced all that Disney has to offer.

Often we enter the doors of the church and become satisfied, with no desire to go further. True, for many of us just coming through the doors is a great accomplishment! But if you press deeper, you will understand what Paul was referring to when he said, "God did this so that they would seek him and perhaps reach out for him and find him, though he is not far from any one of us. For in him we live and move and have our being" (Acts 17:27–28 NIV). When we learn to experience God in this manner, God will manifest his attributes through every breath and

Chapter 1: Knowing Wisdom

step we take. One of those attributes is the ability to know and operate in wisdom.

He desires us to possess his wisdom—to distinguish true from false, right from wrong, and dark from light.

In this book, we will use the tool of wisdom to discover what it means to know Jesus, to know love, to know your identity, to know God, to know the secret place, to know vision, to know hope, to know faith, to know waiting, and to know emptiness.

These are what I refer to as the eight principles of discipleship that lead to wisdom. Once we grasp these principles, we will draw closer to God, where he will then point us again to wisdom. "God understands the way to it and he alone knows where it dwells" (Job 28:23 NIV).

CHAPTER 2
KNOWING THE WORD

Chapter 2: Knowing the Word

The waves from the cool blue water christened the white sand where I planted my feet. I was relaxed on the beach, with no worries or concerns, so my attention turned from the seemingly endless blue ocean to the ambiance of the beach. People were everywhere. Some danced in their festival clothing. The children ran around playing piko, their version of hopscotch. The elders watched with approval and pleasure. The scene excited everyone. The aroma of Filipino cuisine floated through the air as I inhaled and exhaled.

My trip was just like I'd envisioned: the geography, the food, the history, and the culture of the Filipino people. I was in the home of my ancestors. No longer reading a book or listening to my Uncle Brazelle attempt to explain to me the beauties of this graceful land, I was now experiencing it in the flesh. The moment was perfect until, suddenly, an eerie sound began to echo from the endless blue ocean.

I wondered if this sound was a tsunami warning. The people began to scream and run about, confused and scared. The music no longer played, the dancers were gone, and the aroma faded. Everything transformed to black in a flash. I no longer stood but lay flat on my back. I rubbed my eyes to push away the darkness that now suffocated my vision.

For a few moments, the annoying sound was all that any of my senses could grasp. Then, with jarring reality, my vision came into focus and became fixed on numbers. Those numbers were six-zero-zero, or six o'clock. That eerie sound was just the alarm clock. I quickly came to the realization that it had all been a dream.

To visit the Philippines is one of my lifelong dreams. Maybe it's because of my grandmother, a great Filipino woman. Or maybe the stories and videos that my uncle showed me from his travels inspired this dream. On the other hand, it could be from all the research I have done on the culture of the Philippines. Maybe it's even a combination of the three. For a time, I considered myself an expert on Filipino culture. However, one day I encountered a young Filipino lady visiting the United States who proved me wrong. After a roughly thirty-minute conversation, she

Chapter 2: Knowing the Word

told me I knew just enough about the Philippines to get me in trouble.

Have you ever believed you were an expert on a subject only to realize there was much more to learn? Growing up as a believer in my parents' house, I constantly found myself in Bible studies, revivals, and Sunday services. We even held our own services at home. This gave me a solid foundation in my convictions. However, when problems mounted in my life, questions grew. At one time, I asked basic questions: Where is God in my life? Does he love me? Why is the Word not working? Is God leaving me hanging? Am I misinterpreting the Word?

It gave me chills to even ask such questions. I looked to the sky in fear, praying I wouldn't be struck with lightning because of my doubts. But these questions placed me on a journey I never imagined I would take—the journey of truly knowing the Word.

ABCs of the Word

It was the year 1994. I had spent more than half of my life knowing God. However, I began to desire more: a deeper, more intimate relationship with the Father.

To draw near to God, I thought I needed to be a better Christian. One minister on television came to mind about this issue. I remember watching in amazement as he quoted verse after verse with no hesitation. That was my image of what a better Christian looked like. I envisioned having the same knowledge of the Word of God that this evangelist possessed. But where could I find time to memorize Scriptures? My schedule was already swamped with church and playing video games. Then, with a jolt of revelation, I realized I could memorize them at work. I had one of the most important jobs at the college. If I missed work, everyone would notice. The trash would pile up, and the aroma from the bathroom would begin to linger. But being a custodian at a nursing school allowed for plenty of time to think. While cleaning toilets and emptying trash cans, I recited verses over and over in

Chapter 2: Knowing the Word

my mind. That habit riveted such truths deep inside me.

Reciting these verses served as another layer to my foundation of faith. Soon I could quote Scripture just like the minister on television. I found myself in Sunday service reciting Scriptures in my head before the pastor could read them from the pulpit. My knowledge of the Word became so evident that I began to minister at the city mission and other community centers throughout the city.

As time passed, my spiritual endeavors grew. A powerful church had grown out of California, one that was making disciples. Eventually they found their way to my backyard in the inner city of Kansas City. I worked as a servant of God in the inner cities of Chicago, Indianapolis, and St. Louis. While in Indianapolis, I assisted with a church plant. For hours each day, I preached the Word in the streets. From neighborhood to neighborhood and soul to soul, we ministered by providing the Word, food, and shelter.

Finally, our time drew near to leave Indianapolis. Our goals had been reached. An elderly lady approached me and said, "Why are you leaving? We need you here." Up until that point, I had never felt so needed in my life. Yet it was time to move on; there were other cities and people who needed hope.

The years passed, and my love for God and ministry only grew. Yet in the shadows of my mind lurked a seed that began to take root. I knew there was more of God that I had yet to tap into. But what was this more that I longed for?

At the time, I couldn't place my hand on it. Whatever this feeling was, I knew memorizing more Scriptures would not remedy my problem. Have you ever lost something, searched for it, and couldn't find it? Then, sometime later while you're not even looking for it, it appears. This is what happened to me one Sunday. My mind began to open to the solution to my problem at a moment when I wasn't looking for it. It happened during

Chapter 2: Knowing the Word

testimony service. On this particular Sunday, we had a visiting pastor. He was an older gentleman from a much larger congregation than ours. He stood up and began to give his testimony. He said, "Every year, the week before Easter service, we spent hours rehearsing." The visiting pastor described how he would stagger down the center aisle with the cross. His knee problem helped make the staggering convincing, since he used crutches for his bad knees! Every element of that Sunday was scripted. The cross was positioned so the stage lights would cause it to glow and create a beautiful reflection. The music that emanated from the rafters inspired the congregation. He knew his mission was accomplished when he scanned the audience, watching the tears flow from the biggest, toughest man to the youngest children. It was just like he planned. He would do this year in and year out. However, what he said next surprised me.

He said, "It was nothing more than a show." To him the resurrection was just as believable as the Easter Bunny. He went on to say he wasn't sure Jesus even existed.

I couldn't believe it! The pastor of such a large congregation visiting our little church, telling us he was living a lie. The story gets better, though. One day, while he was preparing a message, something happened that wasn't rehearsed. God spoke to him. He never said if it was an audible voice. But he said that at that moment, God opened his eyes and revealed something more. The pastor said he repented and accepted Christ. God healed him spiritually, mentally, and physically. He brought his crutches to church as proof! Resurrection Sunday was never the same for him or his congregation. It was no longer a show but a passion.

This testimony caused me to develop a theory. I had never doubted the existence of Jesus. I *did* doubt his willingness to intervene in my life. My theory was that there are people who have a great understanding of the Word of God. They can tell you a Bible story and reference several verses; they can tell the year each book was written, who

Chapter 2: Knowing the Word

the author was, and maybe even what transpired at the Nicene Council. These people have an academic or head knowledge of the Word of God. But some individuals want something more. These quote Scripture and can tell you many things about the Word of God, similar to the first group. However, unlike the first group, their focus is beyond academia. What distinguishes the groups is a *passion* for the Word, or what I refer to as a heart knowledge of the Word of God.

Today, the church is dealing with a spiritual epidemic. Scholars across the globe are graduating with their big PhDs from theology schools and seminaries. Their knowledge is incomparably greater than almost any before them. Greek and Hebrew are like their second languages.

They teach biblical history and geography as if they've experienced it. Yet they're missing the more.

We can never be satisfied with simply knowing facts. Memorizing a Bible verse and knowing Greek and Hebrew can be compared to a child memorizing the alphabet. It's elementary, only the beginning. Scholars create awesome works of research in dissertations. These dissertations are made up of paragraphs. The paragraphs are created from sentences. The sentences are developed from words. Finally, the words are formed from the ABCs, the foundation. The same is true of the Word of God. If you want that something more, you must move beyond the ABCs of your faith. If you desire to move from the Genesis to the Revelation of the Word, you must not be satisfied with a head knowledge of the Word of God.

Head Knowledge

Allowing us to learn from others' experience is one of the main reasons why the Word was written (1 Corinthians 10:11). So let's look at those who have walked the

Chapter 2: Knowing the Word

earth before us who possessed only a head knowledge of the things of God and see what we can learn from them.

My first example is that of the infamous sons of Sceva, from the book of Acts. These brothers traveled around attempting to cast out demons. They may have witnessed Paul in action or simply heard that Paul the apostle possessed the ability to cast out demons by using the name of Jesus.

These men had good intentions. They encountered a man who was demonically possessed. Obviously, they saw that he was in need of deliverance. They believed they had the knowledge to deliver him.

After all, they knew the magic word! They might have heard that everything was subjected to Jesus' name (Philippians 2:10). So they commanded the demon to leave the man. Their exact wording was, "In the name of the Jesus *whom Paul preaches*, I command you to come out" (Acts 19:13 NIV).

Now, according to what they understood, the demon should have departed from the man. However, the evil spirit didn't follow the script. Instead, it said, "Jesus I know, and Paul I know about, but who are you?" (Acts 19:15 NIV). He turned on them, and the seven sons of Sceva went sprinting down the street naked and bleeding. How embarrassing!

What was the problem? The answer is found in their words. These brothers knew enough about the Word of God to get them in trouble. In Act 19:13, they said, "In the name of Jesus whom Paul preaches" (NIV). They were operating on "he said/she said" basis. They had an academic knowledge of God but nothing more.

Acting on academic knowledge only is like me attempting to mimic my father's cooking skills.

My father is a historian. Before he was a historian, he was a chef. Not just any chef—a five-star chef. Just thinking of him preparing a meal makes my mouth water. One day I hungered for one of his famous meals. Unfortunately, he was on a business trip. I decided to take matters

Chapter 2: Knowing the Word

into my own hands. I made a quick trip to the grocery store, purchased the necessary ingredients, and began cooking tuna casserole. I made sure I used everything he used, down to the same brands.

After an hour of cooking, the meal was ready. I sat down to eat this tasty treat. However, it quickly ended up in the trash. I had done everything I'd seen my father do but didn't get the same results. Later on I asked him what the problem was. There were several issues, but the main one was that I was just going through the motions; there was no passion. As I prepared the meal, my focus was on the final product. I had looked at the preparation steps as nothing more than a to-do list when I should have added each ingredient with love and purpose.

Once my brother and I were over at a friend's house eating spaghetti, and my brother said, "Someone put their foot into this." He could taste nearly every ingredient. It was made with love, not routine.

I have made so many mistakes cooking meals that nearly everyone in my life could tell you a story—there are enough to fill a book! With food, generally it's all fun and games, but missing something in the spiritual world—the ingredients or passion needed to really make something work—is detrimental.

It's easy to think of ourselves as being superior to the sons of Sceva, but we forget that we too have been unsuccessful when trying to defeat the Enemy. Maybe we have never been naked and bleeding, physically tearing down the street and screaming, but spiritually we have been in much the same position.

So let's not boast in their error because the saddest part of this story is that not only were they defeated, but the person they were trying to deliver remained in bondage as well. What causes us to be defeated when we know the Word? They had an academic knowledge, so what was missing? To unlock this question, we will analyze the Pharisees and the Sadducees. Not even today's biblical scholars have a knowledge of the written Word like

Chapter 2: Knowing the Word

the ancient Pharisees and Sadducees had. Though every Jewish man was required to have a thorough knowledge of the written Word, the Pharisees' and the Sadducees' knowledge towered over all others. Still, they had a legalistic view of the Word, emphasizing the letter of the law and ignoring the spirit of the law.

This is why Jesus condemned their teachings (Matthew 16:6). They knew their spiritual ABCs and could quote them backward. However, they did not, nor did they want to, find out the more.

When it came to knowing the Word, the Pharisees and Sadducees were spiritual adults in their own eyes—yet their seeming maturity masked a deep lack. Sometimes we have to unlearn what we have learned. This is what Jesus taught. He said that unless we change and become like little children, we will never enter the kingdom of heaven (Matthew 18:3).

This doesn't refer to literally becoming young but to humbling yourself. A child is more willing to learn than an adult. Often, we as adults will not ask questions because of pride. My three-year-old nephew asked me why my hair is so long. I responded, "Because I do not cut it." He then asked why I didn't cut my hair. I said it was because I like my hair. He then asked, "Why do you like your hair?" On and on . . . because he wanted to know these answers, he kept on to get to the heart of the matter.

He wasn't satisfied with my first explanation. God wants us to come to him with the same attitude. Nothing is wrong with the first question, but we must keep on asking and getting understanding (Proverbs 4:7).

Unless we are willing to admit that we are children when it comes to knowing the Word, our journey into spiritual maturity will never begin. Jesus cautions his disciples by saying, in effect, "Watch out for these guys because they don't know the Word like I know the Word." Additionally, in Matthew 15:8, Jesus says "These people honor me with their lips, but their hearts are far from me" (NIV).

Chapter 2: Knowing the Word

The Pharisees and Sadducees could quote Scripture after Scripture. But because of their own hearts, they were unable to turn those ABCs into concepts and truths that could help them live better lives.

A Heart Knowledge

David wrote in Psalm 119:11, "Thy word have I hid in my heart that I might not sin against thee" (NIV). During the life of David, much of the Old Testament was yet to be completed, and the entire New Testament was yet to be written. But David spoke of hiding the Word in his heart. What did David mean by that?

Hiding the Word in your heart is a little like the game hide-and-seek. The purpose of this game is to find a hiding place. This hiding place must be able to conceal your entire body and even your shadow.

Once you find this place, you shouldn't move. Otherwise you might give yourself up to the seeker. The winner of the game is either the one with the best hiding place or the seeker who finds you. David spoke of a place to hide the Word where the devourer couldn't find it. This place is in the heart. When he fought Goliath, the Word was in his heart.

David was not quoting a Scripture he had just read from the Torah but from what was in his heart when he said in 1 Samuel 17:45–47:

> You come against me with sword and spear and javelin, but I come against you in the name of the LORD Almighty, the God of the armies of Israel, whom you have defied. This day the LORD will deliver you into my hands, and I'll strike you down and cut off your head. This very day I will give the carcasses of the Philistine army to the birds and the wild animals, and the whole world will know that there is a God in Israel. All those gathered here will know that it is not by sword or spear that the LORD saves; for the battle is the LORD's, and he will give all of you into our hands. (NIV)

Chapter 2: Knowing the Word

He quoted from his own heart, where he hid such truths. This is how he was able to write all those beautiful psalms. But how was this possible? Was David just making up words as he went along? No. David fought with more than a sling and five smooth stones; rather, he fought with the unwritten Word he had hidden in his heart. These words David spoke to Goliath were words of prophecy, a declaration of what was to come. What was in his heart was a seed of what was to come. Of course the Father planted these words in his heart. Eventually they became the written Word.

Unlike David, we take the written Word and declare it with our actions. It is then, only then, when we can truly know what it means to hide the word in our hearts. I have seen in my life where I and others have spoken a Word from God, and there is no place where that wording is found in Scripture.

Several years ago, the government conducted a study for land mine detection. This study would pay a reward of $2,000 to those who were involved. The subjects wore land-mine-detecting equipment, searching for items in an open field. However, there were three requirements needed to participate. The first was age, which I qualified for. The second requirement was good health, which I qualified for once again. The last requirement was to pass a math test.

My wife, sister, and I all decided we would take advantage of this opportunity. We thought it would not only be a great opportunity to put cash in our pockets but also to help our soldiers. We headed to the facility to take the exam. My sister, a math major, was confident and had no problems with the test. However, it was a challenge for me. The last math course I had taken was over five years before. (And I only passed that course because I had the help of Skittles and popcorn as visual aids. There were no popcorn or Skittles for this test.) My wife, however, followed the formula of David. She didn't quote a Scripture from her Bible, but she said that she would pass that test

Chapter 2: Knowing the Word

and gave glory to God. A few days later, we received the test results, and it was as she said: she had passed. I was only left with the hope that she would share some of the bounty with me.

I say this only to explain that when you have a heart knowledge of the written Word, no problem, no thief, nothing can steal it away from you. Goliath was probably aware of the power of the Word of God. This may be why he attempted to defuse it with his own words. However, he was unable to move David. Similar to David, Joshua and Caleb hid the Word in their hearts so deeply that generations of giants, the wilderness, forty years, and even their own brothers and sisters were unable to destroy the promise, the word from God prophesied to them. What was in their hearts was even bigger than what their physical senses saw. This is what Paul refers to as believers being living epistles read among men (2 Corinthians 3:2). When we become living epistles, we respond like David did when he fought Goliath or when he wrote the Psalms. In your heart stands a living Word not written in the Bible but just as powerful. There is Scripture within you that even Paul has not written. There is a song within you just as powerful as David's that is not recorded in the book of Psalms. However, we must always search and look to the written Word for confirmation lest we be deceived.

The other day I had several problems conflicting me. I needed money for four new tires, a close friend was in need of a physical healing, and another friend was behind bars. Like David, I was facing a giant. My heart turned toward my heavenly Father. I prayed before the Lord. I said, "Father, become more real to me than the chair I sit on. Let your glory shine through me so bright that the sun is darkness to me." With this prayer, I was declaring the written Word of Isaiah 60:2: "See, darkness covers the earth and thick darkness is over the peoples, but the LORD rises upon you and his glory appears over you" (NIV). The amazing thing was that I prayed this prayer before I knew that Scripture!

Chapter 2: Knowing the Word

Within each one of us, hidden, is the Word waiting to be unlocked. It's like hearing a minister preach and say something so profound that your spirit immediately agrees with it. It's because your spirit already knows and has an understanding you have yet to unlock. But the time for unlocking the Word in our hearts is now.

We are constantly bombarded by circumstances and words that attempt to steal, kill, and destroy the Word we have within us. It might be a doctor's report, a bill, a pink slip, something you read in the newspaper, or maybe words from the lips of a loved one. These things testify against the Word, but if we can get it in our heart, our journey begins and we will overcome by the words of our testimony (Revelation 12:11).

Developing a Heart Knowledge

How do we develop a heart knowledge? Paul and James give us the key by describing the written Word as a mirror.

What is a mirror? Freedictionary.com defines a mirror as something that faithfully reflects or gives a true picture of something else. When you look at the mirror, you don't see the mirror; you see an array of lights emanating from objects in front of the mirror. Likewise, when we look at the written Word, what we are actually seeing is the Word reflecting what is already in us. The apostle Paul says in 2 Corinthians 3:18, "But we all, with unveiled face, beholding as in a mirror the glory of the Lord, are being transformed into the same image from glory to glory, just as by the Spirit of the Lord" (NIV).

One key to developing a heart knowledge is to know that once you have become saved, you are complete in Christ. However, you must also realize that you are being transformed into the image of Christ.

Let's explore more of how the mirror works. The mirror, or written Word of God, reflects your eternal image. This is why Jesus instructs us to be perfect as our heavenly Father is perfect: from God's perspective, we're already perfect. Being perfect is not something we do but a gift

Chapter 2: Knowing the Word

we are returning to God. The same is true of holiness. We don't earn holiness, but we return holiness to God through our actions. When we return perfection, we are allowing the Holy Spirit to move through us. There is nothing you can do within yourself to be perfect; it comes from above.

From our vantage point, we are growing into perfection and holiness. It's like the family picture on my refrigerator. In this picture stand my father, my mother, my older sister, and I. When my friends come over, I show them this picture. They all ask the same question: who is the baby, and who is the girl?

The first couple of times, I didn't understand why they asked that question. Then I realized something: you see, in the picture, I'm the baby, my sister is the girl, and of course, the older people in the picture are my father and mother.

Dad, Uncle pictured above to the far left. My son and me pictured to the right.

However, my friends do not realize I was the baby. At my present age, I look much like my father, and my mother still looks the same, so they mistake my father for me in that picture.

That picture was taken over thirty years ago, and I have been transformed into that same image. The crazy thing was that even when I was a child, people would say I looked just like my father. It's the same with our relationship to Christ. When we first become saved, there is no doubt in God's mind that we will look like him.

As the years pass, he transforms us from glory to glory—we look more and more like Christ. A day will

Chapter 2: Knowing the Word

come soon when people will be unable to distinguish you from Christ (2 Corinthians 3:2).

However, you will not just grow into that image because you accepted Christ and know the written Word. It takes more than reading, memorizing, and men's religion; you have to execute what you know (James 1:22–25). We must behold his Word. An example of beholding is when you observe the written Word with your life, much like you observe holidays. For example, one of my favorite holidays is the Fourth of July. There is so much to enjoy: Fourth of July barbecue, fireworks, friends, family, and more barbecue! When you participate in these festivities, you are observing the Fourth of July. Even so, when you participate in the commands and promises of God, you are observing his Word.

Another form of beholding is meditating. God told Joshua to meditate on the Word (Joshua 1:8). That word *meditate* in Hebrew is siyach, which means to consider, deliberate, and reflect.

When I first heard the word *meditate* in connection with the Bible, I immediately began to stereotype the meaning. In my mind, I had a vision of a monk with his legs crossed on a mountain, chanting with mystical music playing in the background. Meditation is a tool often overlooked by the church because of its association with occult practices. Many forces contrary to God have tapped into it. But that doesn't make it evil in and of itself. A car can be used as a getaway for bank robbers or by a husband driving his wife to a hospital to give birth. Meditation can be used for evil or to bring us nearer to God.

The practice of meditation involves simple steps that can be difficult to master. We will cover the topic of meditation in greater detail in the "secret place" chapter. However, because it is so central to developing a heart knowledge of the Word, I want to take a look at meditation in action here.

As I read the story of David and Goliath in 1 Samuel 17, I imagined sitting in the valley and watching the action.

Chapter 2: Knowing the Word

It was as if I were there. I envisioned David selecting the stones for his sling. My mind began to wonder what the weather was like. Was the wind blowing, or was it hot and humid? I could feel the thud in my spirit as Goliath took a great fall. Then I imagined the giants in my life and how applying the written Word would also lead to their defeat. True, I have never faced a giant quite like Goliath. But we all have faced some sort of giant. It may be your boss or a loved one. Giants come in many shapes and forms. Maybe it's a health problem, physical or mental. I sat in my room journaling as I reflected on overcoming a particular giant in my life. The particular giant I envisioned overcoming was doubt.

Doubt is an indistinct giant, one we tend to view as a reflex rather than as something that needs to be conquered. As an example, have you ever applied for a job and doubted you would receive a call for an interview? You see how doubt is a reflex? Nevertheless, doubt is a giant. David's brothers and the king doubted his ability to slay Goliath. Their doubt played out in initially discouraging David from entering the battle. Doubt has prevented me from believing I qualify. But as I meditated on what caused David to overcome doubt, it helped me. David said, "Is there not a cause?" (1 Samuel 17:28–30 NIV). He overcame doubting thoughts by his focus on the name of God. Goliath was defying the name of God. That is what motivated David.

The fruit of my meditation soon became evident in my life. While I was working for the university in the library, two positions in another department became open. One position was similar to what I was already doing, and the other was a director's position. Doubt almost caused me to apply for the similar position because I wasn't sure I was able to perform what was required for the higher position. I questioned myself. Could I lead an entire department?

Chapter 2: Knowing the Word

How about manage a $300,000 budget? Did I have the knowledge to manage my time wisely? The similar job would only involve a change of location, not position. I was confident in my ability to do what was familiar and sure to me. But doubt tried to prevent me from applying for the director's position. This giant would have prevented me from a big promotion if I had followed it! However, I did not allow doubt to overtake me. I applied for the director's position and received it. Meditating on the passage about David and Goliath allowed me to have victory over my own doubt. This is only a small example of what happens when the Word becomes reality through meditation. Even greater things than this await both you and me.

This is how you move beyond the ABCs of studying the written Word of God: you meditate on it and apply it to your circumstance. The written Word becomes more than historical facts or great stories to tell your children. The Word becomes alive and sharper than any two-edged sword (Hebrews 4:12). To gain a true heart knowledge, it's not necessary to understand Greek, Hebrew, Aramaic, or even English, for that matter! It is based on our willingness to allow the Holy Spirit to teach our hearts.

In Luke 24:13–32, we read about two men named Simon and Cleopas. These men are talking about the death of Jesus, and suddenly a strange man approaches them. The men go on to explain to the stranger what they have heard concerning the events in Jerusalem. With great detail, they tell of how the rulers sentenced Jesus to death. They also speak of the women who saw the empty tomb and angels. After hearing their story, this strange man explains to them how these events fulfilled Scripture. When the strange man finishes his story, the men's eyes are opened to know it is Jesus who stands before them. These men, probably without pencil, paper, or any audio record-

Chapter 2: Knowing the Word

ings, recorded Jesus' words deep within themselves. They developed a heart knowledge, not through tedious study but through yielded hearts. Actually, I like the phrase they used to describe heart knowledge. In verse 32 they asked each other, "Were not our hearts burning within us while he talked with us on the road and opened the Scriptures to us?" (NIV).

What does it mean to have a burning heart? It's not only the warm feeling you get when your hair rises up or you get goose bumps. Having a burning heart or heart knowledge involves taking it to the next step, like the writer of Psalm 39:3 who says, "My heart grew hot within me, and as I meditated, the fire burned; then I spoke with my tongue" (NIV). Speaking and declaring the written and prophetic Word will guide you into developing a heart knowledge.

Amazing things can happen when we have a true heart knowledge of God's Word. I have a few aunties who have used their heart knowledge to develop a gift that the prophet Elijah possessed. In 1 Kings 1:17, we read, "Now Elijah the Tishbite, from Tishbe in Gilead, said to Ahab, 'As the LORD, the God of Israel, lives, whom I serve, there will be neither dew nor rain in the next few years except at my word'" (NIV). Similar to Elijah, my aunts have prayed the rain away at several family cookouts. It's because when they heard the story of Elijah shutting up the rains, they allowed that story to be hidden in their hearts. Not only did they believe it, but they applied it as they spoke it into their own lives. Paul encourages all believers to speak the Word in 2 Corinthians 4:13: "It is written: 'I believed; therefore I have spoken.' With that same spirit of faith we also believe and therefore speak" (NIV).

Just think, God has even more to offer than praying away the rain. Which one of you would like to walk on water? Not just figurative water but physical water?

How about opening the eyes of the blind? With God, all things are possible.

Chapter 2: Knowing the Word

These, I believe, are only the tip of what Paul refers to when he speaks about moving into spiritual maturity. Hebrews 6:1 says: "Therefore let us move beyond the elementary teachings about Christ and be taken forward to maturity" (NIV). God requires maturity of his church so we can manifest our destiny. There is a destiny for you of walking in the power of the prophets of old; even greater works than Jesus performed await you (John 14:12).

But of course, all of this power would be in vain without love. In the next chapter, we will look at the principle of knowing love.

CHAPTER 3
KNOWING LIGHT, LIFE, AND LOVE

Chapter 3: Knowing Light, Life, and Love

The stench penetrated my skin. I felt like I was one of them. It wasn't like this once. I had it all: the finest clothing, exotic foods, transportation, and housing. Now look at me. I have lost it all, and I stink. I can't take much more of this. But what else can I do? I have no other skill, since I spent most of my life living off my father's fortunes. I have no money or friends. I'm stuck here. My stomach is growling uncontrollably. I'm so hungry. But there is nothing here to eat.

Wait a second. Maybe I could eat . . . these. It's better than nothing. Surely it will fill my hunger. Plus, no one will notice. Pig food cannot be that bad; after all, they're still living after eating these pods!

No, I can't, this is just not right. Even my father's servants eat better than this! I know what I will do. Go home and confess my wrongdoings. Surely my father will have mercy on me and allow me to come back as a servant so I can eat.

This is the beginning of the story of the prodigal son, found in Luke 15. Before we complete this parable, let's pull out some of the main elements of the story. This parable gives us a beautiful illustration of God's love. There are three characters here: the father and two sons. The father represents a loving God. Jesus told this parable to give his disciples a vivid example of how God's love works in real life.

Scripture says that God is love and loves all (1 John 4:8, Romans 5:8). But what is his love? There are four Greek words for love. *Eros* is defined as impulsive and sensual love. *Philia* is brotherly love, used several times in Scripture. (One example is found when Lazarus's sisters sent word to Jesus, saying, "The one you love/*philia* is sick" (John 11:3 NIV). *Storge* is affectionate, familial love, like a parent might feel for a child. Finally, there is agape. *Agape* is God's kind of love, unconditional, eternal, never-changing. This is the love we see in John 3:16.

There is a power associated with love that goes beyond definition. We know the beautiful feeling of what it means

Chapter 3: Knowing Light, Life, and Love

to be loved. Even a plant can feel the love of its owner who waters and cares for it. What about the love a mother has for her child, or the love I have for my son and other loved ones? Love is energizing. It causes a desire within us to be around the person who loves us or the person we love. God's love is what gives us our destiny. Faster than the speed of thought, God sends out his love toward us. If we yield to it, we will feel the warmth that surrounds us. If God had withheld his love, his Son would not have come to the earth (John 3:16). Think about the horrible feeling of not having love in your life. Have you ever felt lonely around a holiday or special date? This is a sad feeling, a feeling of being alone in the world even though you may be in a room full of people. Now magnify that feeling times infinity. That's how you would feel without the love of God. The world would be a purposeless place, a place that lacked destiny. Without the love of God, we would be no better than a collection of rocks. But God has demonstrated love to us by sending his Son.

In our lives, the challenge for us is to apply love in everything we do. Without love, all that we do is in vain, it is empty. This is what Paul is talking about in 1 Corinthians 13:

> If I speak in the tongues of men or of angels, but do not have love, I am only a resounding gong or a clanging cymbal. If I have the gift of prophecy and can fathom all mysteries and all knowledge, and if I have a faith that can move mountains, but do not have love, I am nothing. If I give all I possess to the poor and give over my body to hardship that I may boast, but do not have love, I gain nothing. (1 Corinthians 13:1–3 NIV)

With love, prophecy, knowledge, and mystery all have purpose. They have meaning. Manifesting your destiny is tied to love. But what is love? In order to have a more comprehensive view of love, I want to analyze it the perspective of what I call the three Ls: light, life, and love.

Chapter 3: Knowing Light, Life, and Love

All three of these words are interchangeable and are manifestations of love. They all manifest the goodness of God from a different perspective.

Let there be Light

The first L is light. How are light and love interchangeable? When there is an absence of light, there is not only darkness but also an absence of love (1 John 2:11). Where there is no love, you find yourself walking in darkness. In the beginning God said, "Let there be light" (Genesis 1:3 NIV). We see light all the time, so it's easy to take it for granted. But we must remember there was a time when this planet was in complete darkness (Genesis 1:2). Scripture doesn't record how long the earth was in darkness. Theologians even debate the timing, guessing it may have been anywhere from days to millions of years. No one really knows.

Nevertheless, for a moment in time, the earth hung in total darkness. Imagine the feeling of looking up to the sky and seeing nothing but darkness—no moon, no stars, and no sun—then looking forward and seeing no horizon. You wouldn't be able to discern up from down or left from right. You see nothing, only darkness. You feel nothing, only confusion. Darkness produces no vision, no purpose, no life, and no direction.

Recently I took a trip to Times Square in Manhattan, New York, one of the most mesmerizing places in the world. It is full of people of all ethnic groups from throughout the world. As I walked down the street, I listened to the sounds. I heard people speaking in English, Spanish, Arabic, Mandarin, and other languages I did not know. Vendors filled the sidewalks, selling souvenirs, clothing, and other curiosities. Police officers were scattered among the crowd, showing their authority and in control of what appeared to be chaos. Yellow cabs clotted the road, weaving and bobbing through the sea of tour buses, pedestrians, and a host of other obstacles. The sound of horns honking vibrated from one side of the

Chapter 3: Knowing Light, Life, and Love

street to the next. The buildings looked like they touched the stars.

Beyond this was the light that makes Times Square so unique. From building to building were billboards of flashing colors, illuminating the whole area. Large jumbotrons were erected on the sides of these skyscrapers. Each screen had a different image and told a different story. Even during the darkest part of the night, Times Square remained bright as day.

Amidst all that was going on, I spotted something odd. I saw a blind man walking down the street with no escort, feeling his way with only his walking stick. I watched him walk nearly a block until he disappeared in the sea that was Times Square.

This blind man could not enjoy the skyscrapers or the light. To him it was only darkness. Yet he navigated his way through the masses as he ambled down the street. Even in his darkness, there was no confusion. He had direction. He had purpose. This blind man walked in darkness in one of the most illuminated places on earth. Yet not even he would be able to comprehend the darkness that once dwelled on this earth.

There was a story recorded long ago of a great man who lost his eyesight (Genesis 27). Knowing his death was near, he asked his favorite son to prepare a special meal. He told his son he would bless him once he fed him. Little did the father know his wife had overheard the conversation, and she sent out her favorite son to prepare this special meal. When this second son returned, the wife cooked up the meal and disguised her favorite as the firstborn. The second son brought the meal and received the blessing. Because of the father's inability to see light, he was deceived into blessing the second son. This shows the power of darkness: it can deceive even a father and his favorite son.

When Scripture refers to darkness, it is more than just the physical inability to see. Scripture points to a deeper truth, to spiritual darkness and its many manifestations.

Chapter 3: Knowing Light, Life, and Love

Scripture uses darkness as a symbol of evil, which we are to fight (Ephesians 6:12). In physical darkness dwells deception to the undiscerning eye, as Isaac, the half-blind father of the story above, learned. But the consequences of walking in spiritual darkness are much greater. This is why Genesis says in the beginning there was darkness. Lucifer, I believe, caused this darkness in the beginning (Ezekiel 28:15). God did not create it.

An angelic rebellion led by Lucifer, one of the archangels, caused a hideous darkness to fill the earth.

Let's dissect Genesis 1:2. This passage says, "Now the earth was formless and empty, darkness was over the surface of the deep" (NIV). However, using the original Hebrew words, this Scripture can be rendered a different way, which reveals a deeper truth. They key here is the Hebrew expression "*Tohu waw bohu*," which is commonly rendered as "was void." However, it also can be translated "became void." Clues from other passages in Scripture reinforce the "became void" interpretation. For instance, in Genesis 1:28 God commands Adam to replenish or refill the earth. Why would the earth need to be replenished or refilled? To me this implies that something had previously filled the earth. This word *replenish* is the same word used by God when he commands Noah and his sons to replenish the earth after the flood in Genesis 9:1. Another very interesting Scripture to support this interpretation is Isaiah 45:18, which reads, "For thus says the LORD that created the heavens; God himself that formed the earth and made it; he has established it, he created it not in vain, he formed it to be inhabited: I am the LORD; and there is none else" (KJV). That word *vain* can be rendered "without form." So if God did not create the earth "without form," how did it devolve to that state?

The scientific evidence of carbon dating and the measuring of the speed of light also give the earth a much older age than the a "was void" interpretation indicates. On top of the scriptural basis for reading the phrase as "became void," this scientific information is just supple-

Chapter 3: Knowing Light, Life, and Love

mental material. The word *tohu* can also be translated "confused," and *bohu* can also be translated "void or empty." The word *waw* can also be interpreted "became." So Genesis 1:2 can also be read like this: "But the earth became disarrayed and empty; and darkness was upon the face of the earth." A teaching that I recommend on this subject is "*Spiritual Realities*" by Henry W. Wright.

The earth now seemed to be a place without purpose or destiny. But God in his mercy said, "Let there be light." There would be two lights: the lesser and the greater light. Light brings order through purpose. One purpose was to separate day from night. One light (the sun) ruled the day, and the other (the moon) the night. Light also serves as a calendar, a way to measure time. Farmers use light to measure the seasons for harvesting and growing. Astronomers also use it to measure how much time has passed. Explorers of the oceans have used it, especially the light of the stars, to navigate the seas. The great astronomers of the past used the stars to guide them to God in the manger (Matthew 2:1–12). These stars, too, helped maintain order. But that was not their only purpose. The stars or lights also formed constellations, divine images displayed in the sky. We know them today as zodiac symbols, but in ancient times they were referred to as the Mazzaroth (Job 38:32). These symbols were not mere human imagination, nor is their origin pagan. They actually have a divine origin (James 1:17).

They all point to the divine. No Scripture gives as beautiful description as Psalm 19:

> The heavens declare the glory of God; the skies proclaim the work of his hands. Day after day they pour forth speech; night after night they display knowledge. There is no speech or language where their voice is not heard. Their voice goes out into all the earth, their words to the ends of the world. (NIV)

Each of these symbols—Sagittarius, Libra, Taurus, and the rest—foretold what was to come. (There is an excellent

Chapter 3: Knowing Light, Life, and Love

book titled *Witness of the Stars*, written by E. W. Bullinger, that goes in-depth on this topic.) Merely glancing at these stars and the constellations, you can come to the conclusion that they are nothing but stick figures, a really cool game of connect-the-dots.

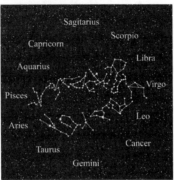

But to the discerning eye, the constellations show the destiny of this planet and everything and everyone associated with it. For example, Sagittarius with its bow points to Scorpio. This is an image of Jesus destroying the enemy. Then there is Capricorn. Capricorn, half-goat and half-fish, represents the church, who have received eternal salvation because of Jesus serving as the great scapegoat sacrifice.

Many ancient cultures were familiar with the signs of the stars. Even the great Mayan civilization understood a message was contained within them. Satan must cringe every time he looks at the stars that point to his soon defeat! But the stars and all of their brilliance are only a shadow compared to him who dwells within you (Colossians 1:27).

So what is the relationship between light and love? John says he who walks in the light loves his brother (1 John 2:10). What does it mean to walk in the light? Does that mean walking only when the sun is out? Or avoiding walking in shady places? No. It means to follow the leading of the Holy Spirit. When you follow the leading of the Holy Spirit, you are not only walking in light but also in love. It's like driving down a freeway with two

Chapter 3: Knowing Light, Life, and Love

names. Occasionally I am following my GPS, and it will say take Route 1, but when I look at the sign, it says Roosevelt Blvd. I question myself: am I going the right way? Of course I am, because occasionally the same street will have two names. I really love how Jesus explains it in John 3:21: "But whoever lives by the truth comes into the light, so that it may be seen plainly that what he has done has been done through God" (NIV). In other words, light is a manifestation of love.

Light also has another purpose. Light encourages growth. Green plants grow from sunlight. Scientists call this *photosynthesis.* Plants convert the energy of light to fuel their development process. At the university where I work, my office had two plants. My assistant, Maggie, took care of these plants, watering them and placing them in the window by the light. I never really paid much attention to the care she gave them. However, one day a better opportunity was presented to her, and she left me to tend the plants on my own. It seemed like it was less than two weeks and those plants were no longer green but dead and brown. I was unsure what I had done wrong, since I watered them frequently. Then it occurred to me—I forgot to place them in the light. This is one of the most important purposes of light: it encourages and grows life.

The church today is maturing not only in terms of quantity but in quality. For too long much of the church has been in darkness. They have lacked light. We see the results by the many deficiencies in the body of Christ. There is a lack of belief, hope, moral behavior, and obligation to the Father. There is a lot of repentance for being caught walking in darkness. But there is not much true repentance to dwell closer to the Father. It is our destiny to walk in the light so the Father may move through us. If we don't, our destiny will be forfeited, and many will be forced to die in the wilderness, blocking them out from the Promised Land.

Chapter 3: Knowing Light, Life, and Love

Living the Life

This leads us to our next L: Life. What is life? At its most basic, life means to exist. Beyond that, though, there is a far more abundant sense of the word. The prodigal son was living, but he didn't have life. Not the kind of life God desired for him.

There was a time when I didn't understand the difference between existing and living. For many years I lived on this earth without life. I wasn't living. I walked around aimlessly, even after salvation. I possessed eternal life, but I didn't possess the earthly victory that goes along with that life (although it was always within reach). Sometimes you don't realize something is missing in your life until something wakes you up to the fact. For each of us, that something missing is different. In some cases we may not realize it until years later. I had recently graduated from high school, a great achievement for someone from my background. Many of my peers had dropped out or been arrested, and some were dead. I was fortunate enough to make it across one of the first hurdles of academia. As a result, I thought I had made it. But life hit me hard. With no purpose or direction, I found myself only existing. My sole purpose was to work all day at a chicken fast-food restaurant and then race home to play video games. That didn't even qualify me to be in the rat race! But one event led me to the path toward life.

At the time, I trimmed hedges in my neighborhood as a second job. As I worked on the hedges one day, I felt like someone was watching me. I looked around and saw a cop car. The officers studied me intensely, but they kept on moving along. Shrugging it off, I continued to trim the hedges. Less then five minutes later, I heard many footsteps rushing in my direction. I looked up, and what I saw scared me straight. In seconds, seven police officers surrounded me. Confused, I wasn't sure what was going on. The only thing I could think was, *Man, I'm about to be the next Rodney King.*

Chapter 3: Knowing Light, Life, and Love

They took the hedge clippers out of my hand and said, "You won't need these where you're going."

My aunt Betty, who lived across the street, heard the sirens and rushed over. The police officer said, "We have been looking for your nephew for a long time." She told the officers they had the wrong guy. After I was able to locate my driver's license and prove who I was, they released me. My life could have taken a bad turn. But thanks to my aunt, I was spared.

The officers left, and the nosy neighbors went back into their houses. It was only me and my aunt outside. She said, "Jamere, you need to do something with your life. Because one day God will come and split that sky and what will you say?" She was right. I thought, *Man, my life is going nowhere quickly.* I wanted a different life but didn't know where to find it. A few months later, I found myself in a men's homeless shelter even though I had a home. In my mind I felt homeless. I felt lifeless. I lived with them for months, ate the same food and worked in the same places. I was searching for life and purpose. I never imagined I would find life in a homeless shelter. I never knew I would find it surrounded by former drug dealers, gangbangers, and prostitutes. But I did.

On the wall in the men's homeless shelter, they had a sign that read "P35." That was the shelter's motto. Anytime anyone got out of line, they pointed to the P35. P35 stood for Proverbs 3:5: "Trust in the Lord with all your heart and lean not to your own understanding" (NIV). I watched men of all ages, all struggles, and all ethnic backgrounds find life through that truth. I saw families restored; men break addictions. For me, it affected me so that I was no longer just living, but I had life. I was used to disappointment. For a long time, I believed that if I just repressed issues, they would not affect me. But in a subtle way they had influenced my very being, my whole understanding of who I was. I would sit in a room with a smile, and what happened around me, whether good or bad, would have no effect on my disposition. I was breathing, but nothing

Chapter 3: Knowing Light, Life, and Love

that life threw at me would affect me much, no matter how horrible or great the situation was. I remember Sunday, during service, that began to change. It reminded me of the Blues Brothers movie when they were in a church service and one of the brothers received a revelation and began to dance. Like them, I began to dance, not only physically, but within my heart. This dance outlasted the beautiful worship music that was playing. It went beyond the four walls. I was alive and victorious.

Peter and Andrew, before their encounter with Jesus, were ordinary fishermen. Their daily routine meant getting their nets, walking into the sea, and casting their nets. They did this day after day. Maybe their father taught them this trade, as it was normally passed down from generation to generation. No doubt Peter and Andrew desired more. But from where?

One day while they were fishing, Jesus came their way and said, "Follow me and I will make you fishers of men" (Matthew 4:19, KJV). They didn't hesitate. Setting aside everything, these men went on to perform many great exploits for God. They walked on water, healed people with their shadows, and witnessed the feeding of the five thousand. They had what Jesus calls the "light of life" (John 8:12, NIV). John also says, "We know that we have passed from death to life, because we love each other. Anyone who does not love remains in death" (1 John 3:14, NIV). When love is present, life will eventually manifest. Remember what happen when Christ died on the cross? Death. But love penetrated through death. This manifested life. Many saints arose from the dead on that day. They passed from death to life. Matthew 27:52 says, "The tombs broke open, and the bodies of many holy people who had died were raised to life." This is an example of love manifested in life. Just think, that was only the beginning of what love will do! There are people who are spiritually dead, people with dead parts in their bodies, people who are dead in their minds. God has destined you to speak those things to life.

Chapter 3: Knowing Light, Life, and Love

It is no accident you were born in this generation. Your destiny hinges on light, life, and love (NIV).

Responding to Love

I can't sleep. Where is he? He never was very responsible. But I love him so. I need some fresh air. Let me step out for a second where I can think. I know just the perfect spot. From here I can see for miles. My son, please come home.

The father stood there, looking expectantly. Suddenly, butterflies filled his stomach, and a joy overtook him. He saw his son far off. He ran toward his son, each step filled with love and compassion. When he was within arm's length of his son, he showered him with hugs and kisses. The father was not concerned about all the lost money, nor did his son's stench prevent him from pouring out his care.

The prodigal son said, "Father, forgive me, I am no longer worthy to be called your son. Only make me a servant."

The father quickly demolished those words by telling his servants to bring the best robe, place a ring on his son's finger, and put sandals on his feet. This sent a message to all that no matter what his son had done, he was still the father's son, and the father still loved him the same.

Love manifests itself in different ways. I saw my mother pull a pit bull off her grandson. I witnessed my father shower his grandchildren with gifts. Many of us know what it means to experience a Savior who died so we might have life (John 10:10). Love awaits us all, much like the Father awaited the return of his prodigal son. The key is how we respond to this love.

The older brother's response to love was jealousy and accusation. He said, "Father, you have given him everything, and I have received nothing. I have always obeyed you."

True, the eldest son was faithful. He had worked hard on the farm. Many farmers have to work from sunrise to sunset. The older son said, "I have never transgressed your commandment" (Luke 15:29). His response to the father's

Chapter 3: Knowing Light, Life, and Love

love was the law, and the law brings condemnation (2 Corinthians 3:9). The older son condemned his brother.

The older son viewed himself as unworthy. He said to the father, "You never gave me anything." The father responded by saying, "Son, everything I have is yours" (Luke 15:31). The older son never experienced what the father was so willing to give because he didn't feel worthy. Maybe he felt he didn't work hard enough. Additionally, the older brother was angry, because in his mind, not only was he unworthy, but his brother was even less worthy. It's as if he was saying, "Not only am I unworthy of the father's love, but so are you!"

He was using his own measuring system for them both.

The problem with the older son was that he didn't know how to respond to love. He didn't know the heart of his father. The older brother could have had more benefits than he was taking. He could have had the party, the goat, the robe, and the ring. But something within him prevented him from taking it.

Ask yourself this question: is there something within you preventing you from acquiring the blessings of God? Both of the sons had the same problem when it came to responding to the love of God. Neither the younger nor the older son felt worthy of the love of the father.

Remember what the younger son said to himself: "I am not worthy to be your son, so please treat me like a servant" (Luke 15:19). In spite of being surrounded by such great love and compassion, he felt unworthy, and he manifested that reality in his actions. Many believers feel unworthy because we don't value ourselves. We behave in ways that work against God's blessing because we don't know who God says we are. Often we feel unworthy of God's love, so we will not accept anything related to his goodness. That's why sometimes we feel we don't deserve the best career, spouse, children, or whatever good occurs in our life. But God says his children deserve the best.

My father and mother have always desired the best for me. One of my earliest memories of this was Christ-

Chapter 3: Knowing Light, Life, and Love

mas one year. I was seven years old. There were so many presents for me under the Christmas tree. But I felt like I didn't deserve those gifts. Some of them I wouldn't even play with. I could have had so much more fun. But something in me said I was unworthy.

The great apostle Peter also suffered from feeling unworthy. In Luke 5:4, we read that Jesus had shown his power and love. They caught so many fish at Jesus's command that their boat began to sink. How did Peter respond? Peter fell down on his knees and attempted to chase Jesus away! He said, "Depart from me, for I am a sinner."

Instead of receiving the blessings with praise and thanksgiving, we often respond like Peter.

We should not respond like the devil responds to God! When the glory and love of God come into our lives, the devil runs.

As children of God, when the glory falls, we should embrace it!

Another occasion occurred in Luke 22. There, Peter denied he knew Jesus three times. Jesus had told him he would do this before the rooster crowed. When his third denial came out of his mouth, the roaster crowed. At that moment, Jesus, standing on trial before the leaders of the Jews, turned and looked at Peter, and Peter remembered what Jesus had predicted. He went off and wept bitterly.

How do you think Peter felt? Once again he had failed. Yet, I bet when Jesus turned and looked at Peter, it was not with eyes of anger and condemnation, but with eyes of knowledge and love. Peter ran because not many people know how to respond to such tremendous love.

On the other hand, consider the disciple John, who called himself "the disciple whom Jesus loved." This disciple wrote that he even leaned on Jesus at their Last Supper. Why is it that the other disciples didn't lean on Jesus? Was it because John was his favorite? No, anyone could have leaned on him. Peter didn't know to do this. But John's response to love was to accept it and let it change his life.

Chapter 3: Knowing Light, Life, and Love

Responding to God is not about what we think, it's about what we know. When God offers something, we should accept. I have a friend who said he couldn't get saved because he wasn't prepared to live a holy life. In a sense, he was right. God loves us infinitely, but often we respond like the prodigal son and spend his love on prodigal living. This is not what God desires. But the truth is that the gift of salvation is for everyone from all walks of life. The gift of salvation is a gift of love (John 3:16).

One thing we must realize about love, holiness, righteousness, and even perfection is that these are all gifts from God that we must accept from him. These are not things we earn or do. You accept the fact that you're perfect (Matthew 5:48). You accept the fact that you're holy (1 Peter 1:16). When you accept these things, they build themselves into your life and give themselves out through you to others. For example, when you accept holiness, you give out holiness in the day.

When you accept the fact that you are righteous, you show righteousness in your life.

You know how the angels in heaven respond to God's gifts? They receive. In Revelation 4:8, it says that the angels call the Lord "holy" and "worthy," and truly he is. Why are they saying this? Is it because God has forgotten who he is? Maybe God is so stuck on himself that he requires them to say it? No. The main reason they say it is because it's true. When you stand in the presence of God, you can only speak truth. However, with God there are also many benefits. When the angels ascribe these attributes to God, they also produce them in their daily living. So when they tell the Lord how holy he is, they begin to show holiness in all they do. When they bless the Lord, they bless others also.

In the parable of the prodigal son, you know what the father was waiting for? He was not waiting for the son to come back and say, "I want to be your servant." He didn't want to hear talk of favoritism. The father wanted to know if his sons loved him. He wanted to hear them both say,

Chapter 3: Knowing Light, Life, and Love

"I love you, Dad." When we respond correctly to God's love, we can say like John, "I am the disciple whom Jesus loves." This is where you accept instead of trying to earn.

After Jesus died on the cross and came back to minister to Peter in John 21:15, he asked Peter, "Peter, do you love me?" Now be sure that Jesus knows what we are thinking, and he knows what is in our hearts. So why did he ask what he already knew? Because there is nothing that sounds more beautiful to God than to hear his children respond to his love by saying "I love you." How can you say "I love you" to God? For each of us it is different. You can only find the answer within you.

CHAPTER 4
KNOWING YOUR IDENTITY

Chapter 4: Knowing your Identity

The clock indicated only one minute left until the school bell would ring and class would be dismissed. I watched the second hand move from second to second, as if looking at it would make class end sooner.

Finally, the dismissal bell rang, and my learning for the day was over. I was free to go home and play. I quickly loaded my backpack and headed home, about a seven-block walk. Little did I know I was about to enter into a fight. About three blocks into my walk home, out of nowhere a guy came at me swinging. I arrived home with a bloody nose and a group of kids following me. To add insult to injury, the guy who had just humiliated me waited outside my house for another round. My older sister, already home, asked, "What happened?" When I told her, she demanded that I have some pride and finish the fight. There is a principle in the hood as well as in life in general: don't let anyone walk over you. On this day, though, I had no intention of living up to this principle, knowing it would only result in part two of the beatdown.

My older sister noticed my hesitation and then said, "I'm going to beat you if you don't go back out there!" So I took her advice, and as I approached the door, she said, "We have your back."

We are Family

I thought to myself, *Why am I the only one going outside to this beating if she has my back?* To my pleasant surprise, when I got outside, my procrastination had paid off. Everyone must have grown bored and left. The very next day, the school bell rang more quickly than it had yesterday. I packed my bags and reluctantly headed off school property. But to my pleasant surprise, my cousins escorted me home. These were the "we" my sister had referenced the day before.

My sister possessed knowledge I lacked at the time. She knew our genealogy, and she understood our last name connected us with family. In my case, this meant older cousins who had experienced fighting. The moment I

Chapter 4: Knowing your Identity

realized my cousins were escorting me home, something changed on the inside of me. The fearful feeling that had overtaken me when the bell rang vanished. A new confidence came upon me. Even weeks later, my walk was different. Family sent an invisible vibe, daring anyone to mess with me. The point of this story is that knowing my identity not only changed my thoughts toward myself, but it changed my thoughts toward those around me also. It manifested a confidence I had never known. Knowing your identity is a key to unlocking your destiny—giving you direction for the purpose for which you were created.

Who are You?

The Bible gives us story after story of individuals with no knowledge of their true identity and purpose until God unveiled it. At a young age, God made plain to Jeremiah his identity and purpose. In Jeremiah 1:5, God says, "Before I formed you in the womb I knew you, before you were born, I set you apart; I appointed you as a prophet to the nations" (NIV). God drew a mental picture for Jeremiah with words by connecting Jeremiah's identity to his purpose. The image that God gave him showed Jeremiah fulfilling his purpose. However, Jeremiah was confused at the portrayal of himself. He said, "That's not me."

Like so many of us, Jeremiah had an incomplete perception of himself. Imagine Jeremiah looking in the mirror and God asking him, "What do you see?" How would Jeremiah respond? What would his heart tell his lips to say? Though God never asked Jeremiah to look in the mirror and tell him what he saw, Jeremiah did tell God how he perceived himself in Jeremiah 1:6: "Ah, Sovereign LORD, I do not know how to speak; I am only a child." In other words, Jeremiah responded, "I'm not mature or good enough to carry out this command."

Like a master designer, God immediately altered Jeremiah's statement. God said, "Don't say you are only a child . . . but remember what I just told you. You are a prophet to the nations" (see Jeremiah 1:5–7 NIV).

Chapter 4: Knowing your Identity

While so many of us try to tear ourselves down, God constantly attempts to exalt us. He hopes we will see our identity through his eyes (Ephesians 1:18). Our focus is on the tangible. But God is omniscient, and his vision is much clearer than ours. As a result, there is more to you than meets the eye, not because of what you have done but because you are his child.

Lessons from Moses

Remember the prophet Moses, who performed all those wonderful exploits for God in the books of Exodus through Deuteronomy? He confronted Pharaoh, led the Hebrew slaves across the Red Sea, and delivered the Ten Commandments to the children of Israel. The prophet Moses was far from an ordinary man! Yet years before Moses was known as the great Hebrew prophet, he had an entirely different identity.

The book of Exodus tells us that after Moses fled Egypt, he rescued a family of Midianite women from a group of shepherds with ill intentions. When the Midianite women's father asked the identity of their hero, one of them responded as recorded in Exodus 2:19: "An Egyptian rescued us from the shepherds. He even drew water for us and watered the flock" (NIV). This woman identified Moses as an Egyptian. Why was this her perception? Maybe because of his attire. Surely he wore the garments of an Egyptian. Maybe his accent helped shape her perception. By appearance, Moses was an Egyptian born and raised. But deep within, Moses knew there was more to his identity. Years later, this feeling was confirmed.

Theologians say Moses lived in the desert for nearly forty years before his appointment with the burning bush. After forty years in one place, you'd think Moses would call this his home, but in Exodus 2:22 we read, "Zipporah gave birth to a son, and Moses named him Gershom, saying, 'I have become a foreigner in a foreign land'" (NIV). Out of the abundance of Moses' heart flowed confusion and frustration. From Moses' vantage point, he was a man

Chapter 4: Knowing your Identity

from nowhere, living nowhere, and going nowhere. It is often when our wheels are spinning in the mud that God shows up. When Moses fled to the desert, in his mind he was escaping the Egyptians. However, in reality God was drawing him toward his destiny.

    I suspect Moses wanted to know his purpose but was unsure of where to begin. He knocked but felt confused about which door to open. He asked but didn't know who he was asking. Moses possessed what many spend their lifetime seeking: fame, wealth, and health. Yet, in his heart, he counted those as rubbish. It was nothing for Moses to surrender what most of us spend a lifetime trying to gain! Moses fled Egypt in pursuit of the unknown. Could you forsake all you have come to understand for that which is unperceivable to you at the moment?

    Moses went beyond the boundaries of what he understood to be civilization into the desert to seek God. God is looking for another person like this. He searches the earth and the hearts of men. Have you ever eagerly searched the want ads for employment? Circling potential prospects? This is what God does. He searches the heart for a man who will immerse himself in God. Are you willing to lose your identity? What about your house, friends, and family? Jesus encountered a man who kept all of the commandments, but he was unwilling to lose his wealth (Luke 18:23). Sadly, this is the state of many in the world. It's hard to give up the visible for the invisible. It's like a form of death. But if we want to receive, we must give that which we hold dear. This is a difficult step to take—but I encourage you to take it. It all begins with heart surrendered heart to your heavenly Father. If you yield to him in this way, he has so much more to offer you. God's desire for us is that we lose our purpose, identity, and estate. If you are able to do this, you will transpose rags for riches. You will exchange your identity for his. This is the only way we can fulfill our destiny (Romans 13:14).

    Deep down, Moses had a dream similar to that of the great Martin Luther King Jr.: to free his people. God has

Chapter 4: Knowing your Identity

also deposited in each of us a blueprint waiting to be manifested.

While Moses tended the flock in this foreign place, the Holy Spirit began to draw him. Moses walked up the mountain of God, tending the flock as part of his ordinary life. Then something extraordinary happened. The supernatural constantly intertwines with the natural in the life of God's people. The question is, how many of us are able to recognize it? If we sense God speaking to us, how many will move upon it? Moses moved upon it. He could have stayed with his usual routine of tending the flock. But the Spirit beckoned him to come and find out the truth.

The Spirit led Moses to a sight no man has since seen. The very presence of God manifested in an unquenchable burning bush. During that encounter, God confirmed what Moses' spirit already understood. For years, Moses had understood he was a Hebrew (Exodus 2:11). But there remained a disconnect with his true identity in Moses' heart until he encountered God.

Many of us know greatness is within us, but our present situation refutes those thoughts. This is when we need a word to propel us. With this next verse, don't just read with your eyes, but listen with your heart. God says to Moses: "I am the God of *your* father, Abraham, Isaac, and Jacob" (Exodus 3:6 NIV).

This is a very different perspective from when Moses referred to himself as foreigner in a foreign land (Exodus 2:2). Moses didn't merely refer to his physical location: he spoke of his identity and destiny. Moses' inner thoughts played out in his actions. His actions said, "I'm lost, and I need to be found." Fortunately for Moses, and for us, this is the place God wants us all to come to so he can mold us (Isaiah 64:8). On that mountain God began to mold Moses' destiny by revealing his identity.

God says, "I am the God of your father, Abraham, Isaac, and Jacob." Moses had a shadow of this truth already in his heart. But now this shadow began to glow and bring

Chapter 4: Knowing your Identity

his identity to light. Once Moses' spirit agreed with his identity, he knew destiny awaited him, and he became anxious to work it out. Exodus 4:18 says, "Then Moses went back to Jethro his father-in-law and said to him, 'Let me return to my own people in Egypt to see if any of them are still alive'" (NIV).

For many years Moses' identity was connected to being an Egyptian. But as he grew, Hebrews 11:24 says, "By faith Moses, when he had grown up, refused to be known as the son of Pharaoh's daughter" (NIV). Circumstances and people will always try to handcuff our purpose by giving us their image of who they perceive us to be. They attempt to limit us by our education, physical stature, economic status, cultural background, or any other tool available to imprison us. But Scripture says in 2 Corinthians 10:5, "We demolish arguments and every pretension that sets itself up against the knowledge of God, and we take captive every thought to make it obedient to Christ" (NIV).

In my life, I had to refuse to be another statistic in the hood. I also had to refuse the doctor's report. I remember it like yesterday. Life was only beginning for me—I had to be about eleven years old. My mother had been concerned about my health, so she took me to the doctors. They performed several tests on me. Then they came back with the results. Even at that age, I could tell it was a bad report. The doctor said I had an irregular heartbeat and it could not be fixed. Well, when I received that evil report, it was already too late. You see, I had already had my mind renewed by listening to Kenneth Copeland and Kenneth Hagin. I stood on the promise of physical healing, even when you couldn't see it physically.

About six years later, they were giving us physicals in high school. The school doctor said, "We have some bad news to tell you." I said, "What, an irregular heartbeat?" They said yes. But I still believed. Six more years passed, and I attempted to enlist in the United States Air Force. I passed the academic test, which qualified me for the air force, but once again we had a physical. They said, "You

Chapter 4: Knowing your Identity

don't qualify." I said, "Why? Because of an irregular heartbeat?" They said, "No, your heart beats fine. It's just your curved spine." God had healed me, and he is continually manifesting his healing power in me.

We cannot allow what people say, no matter how qualified they are, to affect our belief in what God has done for us. I continue to refuse anything contrary to the Word of God. I had to refuse the identity the world wanted to place on me. I had to deny what the grades on my transcripts said about my English skills.

I even had to reject thoughts from within myself. The world abounds in knowledge that is contrary to the knowledge of God and his purpose for our lives. The Enemy specializes in flooding our minds with doubt. But Scripture says in Isaiah 59:19, "When the enemy shall come in like a flood, the Spirit of the LORD shall lift up a standard against him" (NIV). So when the Enemy comes and tells me "You can't write a book; just look at your English grade on your college transcripts," I have to fight those thoughts by saying, "My heavenly Father has given me divine language that supersedes anything my transcript says." We must refuse the Enemy and use God's Word to lift up a standard. Our destiny depends on it! Moses refused to be identified as an Egyptian. That refusal resulted in Moses being identified as one of the greatest prophets to ever walk the earth.

Distorted Identity

Knowing your identity, as we observed in Moses' life, can have a great impact on your self-perception. Notice the key word here is can. Just because you know something doesn't guarantee you'll walk in it in such a way that your knowledge brings success.

This is a struggle I faced during my school days. My family constantly moved from school to school and neighborhood to neighborhood. With each move, I found myself in situations where I had to prove myself—not only to those who challenged me, but also to myself. I was

Chapter 4: Knowing your Identity

always different from the others around me. My physical appearance and my personality separated me from the rest. It made me a target to bullies and those who were jealous of me for whatever reason. It became very discouraging, as I had no ability to blend in. Some made fun of me. That can cause you to lose confidence in your identity. The confidence I had possessed as a child left me. It seemed like another lifetime ago.

Gideon also felt like this. He hid from the Midianites because he couldn't connect with his identity. He even referred to being from Manasseh, the weakest tribe (Judges 6:15). Gideon knew a lot about his genealogy. However, he lacked confidence in his present circumstances, which hid the greatness awaiting him. His self-esteem was low. He was orphaned and disconnected. His experience was contrary to the stories told by his ancestors. This is what he told God in Judges 6:13:

"Pardon me, my lord," Gideon replied, "but if the LORD is with us, why has all this happened to us? Where are all his wonders that our ancestors told us about when they said, 'Did not the LORD bring us up out of Egypt?' But now the LORD has abandoned us and given us into the hand of Midian." (NIV)

Gideon wanted to experience the power and miracles of God. He was not lacking faith. As a matter of fact, Gideon is listed in the "Hall of Faith" (Hebrews 11). Gideon's problem was lack of experience. Just like Jeremiah and Moses, Gideon needed to see himself through the eyes of God. So God began to plant a seed in Gideon's heart when he called Gideon, "A mighty man of valor" (Judges 6:12 KJV).

Even after God called Gideon a mighty man of valor, Gideon still had a problem relating that to his life. That's why he continually asked God to confirm what God had already stated concerning his destiny.

Chapter 4: Knowing your Identity

What made Gideon a mighty man of valor? The same thing that gave Daniel the ability to interpret dreams, Samson the strength to slay one thousand, and Joseph the wisdom to prepare for the famines in Egypt. The Holy Spirit was not only with Gideon but also in him. God began to mold Gideon's self-image because Gideon was willing. Are you willing to let God to mold you into his image? We have talked about Jeremiah, Moses, and Gideon. Now it's your turn. Who are you? What is your identity?

Your Identity

It was a nice warm day, and my aunt decided to take us out for a walk. Walking around the block, we encountered one of her friends, and she asked, "What kind of kids are these?" She had never seen us before. Sometimes I ask myself the same question! Of course my aunt could never explain it. But the answer to what kind of kids we were begins overseas. Like many in the United States, I am a mixture of different nationalities, ethnicities, and races. My identity, bloodline, and culture can be traced to the islands of Jamaica and the Philippines—and also to the countries of France, India, Nigeria, and of course, the United States. All of these elements contribute to my identity. But these natural traits within me cannot lead me to fulfilling my true destiny. The same is also true of you.

If you ever want to fulfill your destiny, you must go to your beginning. I'm not simply referring to the country your ancestors are from, what hood you grew up in, or your ethnic background. No, this is something far greater.

In the Beginning

First, let's examine our beginnings. Remember in Genesis chapter 1 when God was creating the world and the things in the world? God called the plants out of the soil. He brought the animals out of the ground. He created the fish in the seas and the birds out of the air. But when God fashioned man, he called man out of himself.

Chapter 4: Knowing your Identity

Your earthly body is merely dust formed from the ground, but the invisible element of you, your spirit, is nothing less than the offspring of God. God said, "Let us make man in our own image and likeness" (Genesis 1:26 NIV), and we are told that God breathed life into the first man.

Not only did you come from God, but you were also designed in his very image. Scripture points to this truth. Jesus says in John 10:34 (NIV), "Is it not written in your Law, 'I have said you are gods?'" What Law or Scripture is Jesus referencing? The passage can be found in Psalm 82:6, which reads, "I said, 'You are "gods"; you are all sons of the Most High.'" Peter alludes to this in 2 Peter 1:4: "Through these he has given us his very great and precious promises, so that through them you may participate in the divine nature, having escaped the corruption in the world caused by evil desires." God molds us for something that only our spirit man can understand.

What then does our spirit understand? If you search your spirit deep within, you will hear what the Holy Spirit is saying, which will be confirmed by the written Word. You will hear the Spirit say you are holy, righteous, royalty, a priest, a member of a holy nation, an ambassador, a soldier in a mighty army, a ruler and judge. These are titles we have heard in songs and Bible studies and seen on bumper stickers. However, in real life these titles seem elusive, fictional, even hysterical in light of our present situation. But we should not feel that way.

For me, it was hard to feel like a king when I was cleaning toilets. The Word said I was a mighty warrior. But when I looked in the mirror with my bloody nose, I only knew defeat. These majestic titles placed on us from God seemed incredible.

Why would God call us something we are not? Why does his truth seem like a lie? It's because he proclaims the impossible. When we hear it over and over again, our attitude sometimes says, "Yes, whatever you say." We laugh hysterically in our hearts, like Abraham's wife, Sarah

Chapter 4: Knowing your Identity

(Genesis 18:12). But we must learn that these titles are real. Eventually Sarah took hold of the title God was trying to give her, the title of motherhood. In Hebrews 11:11 it says, "By faith Sarah herself received power to conceive, even when she was past the age, since she considered him faithful who had promised" (NASB). This is quite contrary from where Sarah started. Many of us face the same destiny. We may start off going backward, but if we yield to the power of God, we will conceive what God has already called done. God has a majestic destiny for you.

Millennium Reign

The titles God gives us, no matter how wild they may seem, are more authentic than any of our current titles in this world. What helped me understand this concept was a glance into our future. When I say future, I'm referring to a time after the tribulation period, a time after the rapture, a time after the war of Armageddon. This time is a period scholars refer to as the millennium, the thousand-year reign of Christ on earth.

During this millennium reign, Satan will be bound for one thousand years in the bottomless pit. Jesus will literally live on earth, ruling it with an iron rod. He will rule with a group called the elect, which is made up of all who have accepted Christ. But who will we be ruling?

During the millennium reign, there will be two types of humans on earth. The first group will be the elect. You and I are the elect, in our glorified state. However, we have another group of humans on earth during this time; these are the unsaved who survive Armageddon. We will govern these people with Christ. Scripture refers to Jesus as the King of Kings and the Lord of Lords (Revelation 19:16). Just a hint: the "kings" who rule with Jesus are not Queen Elizabeth or Barack Obama. This verse is referring to you!

Not only will we rule on earth, but we will also master the universe. Why do you think God made so many planets?

Chapter 4: Knowing your Identity

They are not merely for decoration but to be governed (Ephesians 2:6–7). Additionally, there will be a time when we will judge the fallen angels (1 Corinthians 6:3). All of those menacing spirits that are causing problems in your life already know their fate. Imagine being in the heavenly courtroom, and a fallen angel appears before you. This particular fallen angel is one familiar to you. He is one who caused you much harm and pain in your life. You're in the courtroom, and God asks you what is the verdict. What will you say? You will judge swiftly and righteously (Revelation 6:10).

Governance and Dominion

I have just told you of things that are greatly debated and even controversial. But these topics greatly excite and encourage me. My previous way of thinking was that I couldn't wait until the rapture so these things could transpire. I couldn't wait to go to heaven. Then I heard one teacher say, "Why are we so anxious to go to heaven when our responsibility is to bring heaven to earth?" Though I still desire to be in that great city, I now understand that I have a destiny for here and now. This destiny is to manifest heaven on earth. I'm only echoing what Jesus said in the Lord's Prayer in Matthew 6:10: "Thy kingdom come, thy will be done in earth, as it is in heaven" (NIV). When it's all said and done, God will bring that holy city to earth, as the apostle John wrote in Revelation: 21:10: "And he carried me away in the Spirit to a mountain great and high, and showed me the Holy City, Jerusalem, coming down out of heaven from God" (NIV).

So what is our role in bringing heaven to earth? Like John the Baptist prepared the way for the first coming, we are preparing the way for the next coming. Therefore we must work in the spiritual authority given us by God. Luke 10:19 tells us, "I have given you authority to trample on snakes and scorpions and to overcome all the power of the enemy; nothing will harm you" (NIV).

Chapter 4: Knowing your Identity

We can learn to operate in this authority by examining worldly figures of authority.

Police officers, governors, presidents, and even teachers—all are figures of authority within their own domain. Even children in their domain have a position of authority. When I was a child, I was the authority over my bedroom. My parents gave me this position. Even though the house was in their name, they designated one bedroom as my responsibility. Of course they gave me guidelines and rules, and I attempted to follow them to the best of my ability. Those rules included keeping the room clean and not punching holes in the walls. However, this was one of those cases where the concept of entropy ruled. Entropy means it is inevitable that everything will go from order to disorder. I often had a cluttered room. On occasion, I had friends over who had fewer stakes in keeping my room clean than I did. Oftentimes my room would end up in a mess. I had pancakes sticking on the floor, trash all over the place, etc. It wasn't my parents' doing; they had given me this responsibility to prepare me for greater responsibility in adulthood.

God governs us in this same manner. The earth and everything in it belongs to God (Psalm 24:1). However, he has given it to us: "The highest heavens belong to the LORD, but the earth he has given to man" (Psalm 115:16 NIV). The earth, in a sense, is our bedroom. It's our responsibility to keep it clean; to keep friends, family, and even enemies from destroying it. We are to have dominion over the earth according to Genesis 1:26. Perhaps a better way to grasp our authority is to compare it to Satan's. It is common knowledge that Satan is only a creature, created by the Father. There is no comparison between the two. However, what about us? Are we in the same boat Satan is? We will get a piece of the puzzle from Psalm 8. David composed a wonderful psalm admiring the great universe that God has created. Then he began to look inward and focus on men, and he wrote one of the most debated Scriptures in the entire Bible: "You have made them a

Chapter 4: Knowing your Identity

little lower than the angels and crowned them with glory and honor" (Psalm 8:5 NIV). However, obscured behind the English word "angels" is the word *god*, or in Hebrew, *elohim*. This gives a different perspective on our authority. According to biblical hierarchy, we are ranked lower than God but higher than all angels, including Satan.

Biblical Hierarchy diagram

But what does this mean? On his own, Satan is nothing. The role of angels is clearly stated in Hebrews 1:14: "Are not all angels ministering spirits sent to serve those who will inherit salvation?" We as the children of God are those who have inherited salvation. Satan can only move through us when we yield to him.

A practical example of this is when I served in what we called the few, the proud, and the brave. While in primary education, I served in a position of authority as a public safety officer. I wore my badge with honor and authority, serving in company C. Our mission was to uphold the laws of the school. Every morning before school, you could find me strolling up and down the lines, enforcing safety regulations. Some of my duties included making sure no one cut in line and preventing the students from fighting. A teacher was present most of the time. Their presence confirmed to the other students our authority. Additionally, their presence helped to keep us in check. When we were not outside, we were assigned to door watch. When watching the door, we were to prevent anyone from entering or exiting the building. On several occasions, we had a problem. A group of banned students kept accessing the

Chapter 4: Knowing your Identity

building, waging havoc. After an internal investigation, we discovered that a few of the officers were allowing these students in. On some occasions they would sneak them in, and other times they left the door open so they could come in later. This is how Satan functions.

He uses our authority to sneak in through the back door. This has happened numerous times in Scripture. Jesus rebuked Satan, who was using Peter as a door (Matthew 16:23). This is why Satan will manifest through the Antichrist in the last days (2 Thessalonians 2:8). There is wisdom to be learned from this. Not only do you have more power than Satan, but so do those who are without eternal salvation. I recently heard a testimony of a sorcerer who could control the weather, causing the temperature to drop and even bring a cold, dark rain. Of course wicked spirits are manipulating things in the background. But they only can operate that way because of the person who has yielded his or her authority over to those spirits.

Likewise, this is one of the reasons Jesus was sent to this earth in the form of a man. He became a man to meet God's demand for an acceptable sacrifice for sin (John 1:29) and to take back the authority Adam gave to Satan. God as God *only* could not intervene. Jesus had to become the God-Man. Remember when Jesus was tempted by Satan in the wilderness. Satan said, "I will give you all the kingdoms of the world if you bow to me" (Matthew 4:9). Yes, God is sovereign and in total control; he owns the deed to the land (Psalm 50:10). However, he has given us authority, and whenever we yield to Satan, we allow him to rule. There is something that God gives his sons and daughters that is not clear to man (1 Corinthians 2:9). But this something is something great.

We have yet to fully tap into what God desires to do through us. So we must be encouraged. So far we have connected our identity with our future and even our past. But what about now? What is our identity as the church now? It will be hard for me to explain unless we look at how we arrived at our current position.

Chapter 4: Knowing your Identity

So let's travel back into the past again, particularly to the Middle Ages.

Martin Luther: The Present Church
The invisible stench began to seep through the cracks. Many were unable to detect or even smell the odor. The church was not designed to function in this manner. The blueprints did not match what was constructed. There were many cracks in the foundation. Maybe the others just ignored it, or maybe they too knew something was terribly wrong. As far as the average person could tell, the appearance from the outside was grand and marvelous.

It had grown to be the most influential entity on the planet. Yet deep down on the inside, it was rooted in corruption.

I wasn't sure what to do about this. It ate at me day and night. One day I heard a voice. It prompted me to take actions that would bring division, though that was not my intent. I only wanted truth. I only wanted God. I sat there at my desk with paper and ink, knowing with each stroke of the pen that trouble was near. The conflict not only came from within but from the unseen all around. He was so cunning with his words. There was nothing he would withhold in attempting to stop this divine plan, including placing sickness on me. He gave me no rest day or night. I even came to expect his presence attacking me. Yet I knew he would flee when I sent praises up. I knew his words would become void when I confronted him with the words of God. This was too great a task to let the Devil stop me. Many souls needed to know. We needed renewal. We needed to come out of the traditions and doctrines of men. Finally, after much pain and tears, I was finished. My Ninety-Five Theses were complete.

The year was 1517 when the great reformer Martin Luther nailed his ninety-five arguments to a church door in Wittenberg, Germany. This event triggered the Protestant Reformation. After this, Luther formed the Protestant

Chapter 4: Knowing your Identity

church in Germany, challenging the authority of the pope in Rome. One of the main issues was the Catholic Church setting the pope in higher authority than the Word of God. Other issues of corruption in the church were brought out too. Through Luther and others, many souls began to find spiritual freedom as God called his children out of the traditions of men. The Reformation was not an easy road; it brought division, chaos, and even death to many. But now, more than five hundred years since that event, God is once again calling his people out of the traditions of men. He is calling his people out of denominations, buildings, social clubs. If you heed this call, this voice to take action, you too will possibly face division, even from within chaos, even from within, and death even from within. It's a battle on many fronts, "fleshself" vs. "spiritself," family vs. family, tradition vs. destiny. From mere appearance, it seems you're fighting a denomination or tradition. But the truth is you are fighting to manifest the destiny to which He has called you.

The Called-out Ones

We in the present church often think of "church" as a building. However, the original Greek word for church is *ekklesia*. This word means the "called-out ones." It refers to the people, not to the place where they meet. So what difference does it make? Should you stop calling the building you attend a church? Not necessarily. My desire is that you understand who you are.

Because of how we view the church, there are certain things we will refrain from doing out of reverence for a building. Some of us will limit our vocabulary. Others will change our attire. There are some who will walk a certain way. Some people practice such rituals only because of their physical location. However, once outside the building, almost anything goes. My purpose in saying this is not to judge but to reveal. When you behave in this manner, you only devalue yourself. This is not what your king desires for you. He is more concerned about you than a

Chapter 4: Knowing your Identity

physical location. What convicts you inside the building should also convict you in your bathroom, the club, or wherever you dwell.

This is just one issue the church faces today. We know the church has a list of other problems. Today, many of those come down to one thing: the church is in a place where she should not be. Revelation 18:4 says: "Then I heard another voice from heaven say: 'Come out of her, my people, so that you will not share in her sins, so that you will not receive any of her plagues; for her sins are piled up to heaven, and God has remembered her crimes'" (NIV).

The majority in the church today are in a dry, dead place. One of my pastimes is visiting different churches every time I travel. I sit in the back and watch the actions of the church, though every church does not operate in this manner. The youth sit in the back playing games, adults struggle to stay awake, and others appear perplexed as they look at their watches. These are signs of how irrelevant the church has become to many.

A good portion of the present church is spiritually deficient. This is from my observation in several congregations, particularly here in United States of America. But how can this be? According to various sociological stats, Christianity has just over two billion members. In terms of population, that ranks it number one among world religions. Sociological stats project that this number will continue to grow. These are not signs of a spiritually deficient church. But festering among those numbers is a significant number of spiritually deceived and deficient believers, particularly in Western society.

It is my fear that many who profess to be believers are only members of a building. Even worse, many leaders of the church are leading them down this road of destruction as prophesied by Jesus in Matthew 7:22 (NIV): "Many will say to me on that day, 'Lord, Lord, did we not prophesy in your name and in your name drive out demons and in your name perform many miracles?'" This is my own per-

Chapter 4: Knowing your Identity

sonal theory, but I believe the "great falling away" began centuries ago, and it continues even until this day. I know many have been taught that the great falling away is something that will transpire in the future. But let me tell you this one truth a good portion of Revelation is occurring even before our eyes.

One example that I can give you comes from Revelation 8:11: "the name of the star is wormwood. A third of the waters turned bitter, and many people died from the waters that had become bitter" (NIV). The key word here is *wormwood*. In 1986 the greatest nuclear accident occurred at a nuclear power plant named Chernobyl, but the name can also be translated as wormwood. It is said that this explosion released ten times the amount of radioactive substances that was released by the bombing of Hiroshima in World War II. An immense cloud of radiation would soon infect the world's water supply. This could be the reason so many are dying of cancer. There are other more specific prophecies that Brother Irvin Baxter address that I find very interesting in his "Understanding the Endtimes" series. But let's focus on the great apostasy.

I estimate the great apostasy began somewhere around the year AD 300. This is around the time organized Christianity was established. In a sense, it was a revival of the Pharisees and Sadducees. The legalization of Christianity was led by Constantine, who had a vision of a cross before a battle in which he was victorious. I'm not sure what his intent or motivation was as he legalized Christianity, but as a result he not only took the lives of many believers but also many truths. I'm not saying these ancient Christian sects possessed the whole truth, but they did contribute much to the faith. They knew in part and prophesied in part (1 Corinthians 13:9). However, many were crushed and all but eradicated. This could have been dealt with differently. Right now the dispensation and purpose of God is to love, not to destroy (Luke 9:54), to bring truth and revelation, not to hide it (John 1:17). This spiritual eclipse of the truth was only the inception of the great

Chapter 4: Knowing your Identity

apostasy. Maybe this is why some historians identify this time frame as the Dark Ages, though they may not understand the real reason for their terminology. What I find ironic is that around this same time, Christianity became legalized in Rome. It is often taught that the great apostasy is something that is reserved for the last days. I agree.

But let's look closer at the last days. When did the last days begin? Is it something that will happen within twenty years? Or something that began in 2012? Let's examine Scripture. In Acts 2, Peter even says that he was living during the last days. That was over two thousand years ago. Hebrews 1:2 also confirms that God spoke through Jesus in the last days. I believe the birth of Jesus marked the beginning of the last days. Since that time, much has occurred: the rise and fall of nations, wars, famines, and more deception. Darkness attempts to make its ultimate eclipse in preparation for the coronation of the great Deceiver (2 Thessalonians 2:3). However, he and those who intentionally and ignorantly align themselves with him will face certain doom. We each individually must judge our own hearts and determine our spiritual disposition if we're to escape a place of soon judgment.

In the background of this present darkness, a remnant of God's people remains. With each passing generation, their destiny only unleashes itself in greater measure. This group, though small in number, will spearhead the great harvest foretold by Jesus in Matthew 24:14. In fact, they are already doing it. They will use the weapon of love to penetrate those with hardened hearts and perform great exploits (Daniel 11:32). Many will be presented with a decision of eternity. What is at stake is more than heaven or hell. Will you embrace the ever-loving Creator, or will you ignore such a great salvation (Hebrews 2:3)? This choice will not be an easy one. It will challenge your beliefs, your traditions. Many today are persecuted for believing in such a way. In the West we label them as third-world believers.

Chapter 4: Knowing your Identity

However, they are far from that in God's eyes. They are the greatest in the kingdom. In these remote places, the sword of death reigns in an attempt to prevent the purpose of God. Yet great signs and wonders occur in these lands that confound the rest of the world. As God assembles the host of heaven and the great cloud of witnesses, he is also raising a company in our realm.

Even at this very moment, God is calling us out of the traditions of men. The Father is beckoning us to have true communion with him. He is waiting for us to recognize that, like Moses, Jeremiah, and Gideon, we have been called to walk in a higher realm. All creation is yearning and hoping for the church to take this step. Once we walk through this spiritual door, something powerful will occur. This something powerful will make the day of Pentecost seem like child's play. God has prophesied through the prophet Haggai that "The glory of this latter house shall be greater than of the former, saith the LORD of hosts: and in this place will I give peace, saith the LORD of hosts" (Haggai 2:9). It is essential that you discover the door you must walk through. Martin Luther cracked it. Now, however, we must knock the door off the hinges. You can only discover this door by knowing God—not only an "eternal salvation of the spirit" knowledge, but a knowledge that leads to salvation for every situation you face (2 Corinthians 2:14).

There are those whose traditions and experience give them the perception that God is apathetic in his responses to our problems. A smaller percentage see God as sympathizing with us. Only a minute number believe God actually empathizes with our problems. We must come to the knowledge that God desires to make himself real in every circumstance (Hebrews 4:15–16). Once you come to this revelation, to this understanding, your vantage point begins to change. Once you look up to the hill, the solutions to your problems will manifest themselves: "I will lift up mine eyes unto the hills, from whence cometh my help" (Psalm 121:1 NIV).

Chapter 4: Knowing your Identity

What do I mean by looking to the hill? What specific actions must we take?

The path we take will be different for each of us. I'm not referring to salvation since that is only one way, but I'm referring to situational salvation. Without knowing your background or who you are, there is no specific guidance I can offer. There are no twelve steps However, I can offer you the knowledge that there *is* a door you must walk through. It is not merely looking for a hill to look up. What we are looking for is not a physical door but a spiritual one. For me, this door is unlike any I have ever known. For a long time I searched for this door, first unknowingly but eventually with deliberate purpose. The amazing thing is that it has always been there. Right now, your door is even in the very room where you dwell. I say "door" only to imply that what we are looking for is a passage from the natural to the spiritual. In order to access this passage, you must place yourself in a position of receiving, similar to positioning a satellite dish to receive a signal or walking around to get a clear cell phone signal. As I seek it, I will say something like, "Father, here I am. I thank you for all you have already done and are doing. Father, speak to me in a way I can understand and open my eyes the way you have others." Now, you don't have to say it exactly in that wording, but what is important is your heart's desire. You may not see or hear a thing. But just wait—eventually you will. Once you walk through this door, the Spirit will give you understanding of what is required of you. In the next chapter, we will discuss who waits before you beyond the door.

CHAPTER 5
KNOWING YOUR FATHER

Chapter 5: Knowing your Father

Sitting in the back of the class waiting for my first day of band to begin, I noticed dust everywhere on the musical stands, the chairs, and even the piano. The ambiance of the room gave the impression it was forsaken. I had never been musically inclined. My music resume began with dropping out of piano lessons at the age of nine, though this was not my fault. Every time I hit the wrong key, "the punisher"—the twelve-inch ruler the instructor used to hit my fingers—would come out. Later on in life, the leader kicked me out the choir for singing loudly and off-key. I thought singing in the choir called for singing loudly! I began to second-guess myself. Maybe another elective was available. Maybe an easier course could be taken. But there was no turning back. I had made my choice. Band remained the only path toward graduation.

The seats quickly filled up, and the instructor arrived as these thoughts raced through my head. She scanned the class as she marked us present or absent. She never gave tardies. In her hand, she held a baton for conducting.

Seeing it only made me cringe. I imagined her striking my hands for playing the wrong note.

Most of the students were returning from the previous year, and I stood out like a Bentley among Ford Escorts. The instructor's eyes intensely focused on me as if she wanted to read my mind. She asked me what musical instrument I played as she neared me with that baton in her hand. I thought surely she would whip the answer out of me if I didn't respond quickly.

I went straight to the point. "I play no musical instruments."

"Well, what musical instrument would you like to learn?"

I scanned the room and studied each instrument, hoping one would stand out. Somehow it would say, "Play me." But I couldn't focus—my mind was riveted on the baton.

Chapter 5: Knowing your Father

I didn't want to make the wrong choice. I had thought this class would be so easy, but it felt like a huge test had already begun. Plus, it had never crossed my mind that I would actually have to play an instrument!

The instructor, tired of waiting for my response, looked me up and down with her withering eyes as she walked past me toward the bookshelf in the back. She picked up a book, placed it on my desk, and said, "You look like a saxophone player."

There were only two things I knew about the saxophone: that it was a brass instrument and that Kenny G played it. However, over the next couple of months, the sax became my best friend. The first month dragged. Every other day, the sax made a trip to my house. My friend Marcus, who lived next door, made fun of me as he heard the cacophony of sound reverberating from my bedroom window. I couldn't blame him. I knew the sound was awful. But I wanted to graduate.

As time passed, my mind became the Rosetta Stone of music. Those strange hieroglyphic symbols that I studied were now musical notes that turned into full scores.

After an entire school year exposed to the saxophone, my knowledge of this instrument became obvious as my neighborhood friends no longer mocked me. My performance at school concerts and shows proved my expertise. My fear of the baton also faded. I passed the course, my goal accomplished. I had never wanted to master the sax like Kenny G. I have since put the sax down. If asked today, roughly twenty years later, I couldn't play the saxophone to save my life. I'm left with only memories of how it once was. I used the sax to graduate, but it has had no lasting place in my life.

Many believers treat our experience with God like I treated the saxophone. After being introduced to a loving Savior offering a one-way ticket to heaven, we become self-satisfied. We no longer worry about eternal punishment. When God calls us, we will be caught up in the rapture in the twinkling of an eye.

Chapter 5: Knowing your Father

However, our desire should be to pursue God like a musician pursues his music.

We must continue to know him, to build communion, and not to be lulled to sleep like the Corinthians or Eve (2 Corinthians 11:3).

Our first encounter with God must not be our last. Our first filling of the Spirit must not be our last.

Often, we believers reminisce about what it was like when we first became citizens of a new kingdom. Things were sweeter; we wanted to learn and grow into the deeper truths of God. The teachings of baptism, the Romans Road, and the feeding of the masses brought multiple revelations. The story of the prodigal son brought tears to our eyes. But time passed, and life intervened. Somewhere along the path, we ceased to move forward in God.

This is a path many believers have taken, and few advance past the roadblock. It's not that they don't desire to surpass their current plight. Many have ransacked every possible way they can understand. They have investigated every way out. With no hope, and not comprehending which steps to take, they are bound in disarray. However, they have neglected to examine one central truth. This one simple truth is that God is within us.

Camping with Grandpa

We can compare moving forward into the presence of God to preparing for an expedition or camping trip. When I was a child, my grandfather would take all of his grandchildren camping. Those trips brought great conversation and laughter to family events, including stories of what

Chapter 5: Knowing your Father

went on in the tents at night. Hunting for dinner, scaring my younger cousins, and roasting s'mores are all precious memories I hold dear to my heart. We lacked nothing on those trips. My grandfather prepared everything. I remember helping him load the RV. He brought tents, clothing, hygiene items, food, matches, and a first aid kit. The RV loaded, every trinket and device had its purpose. However, out of all the materials we packed, only a few were essential. We could not have made a trip without them. These were our starting point, our destination, and the map. In the twenty-first century, everything is digital; you only need a GPS. A GPS will show you your starting point and ask you for your destination address. After you enter the data, it will give you a map, directions, and even an intended arrival time.

We have a similar tool for our journey as we press into the deeper things of God. The Holy Spirit will serve as the voice of the GPS.

The Temple of God

The Holy Spirit is our guide to truth (John 16:13). Our map is the temple of God. This map will give us the other two essential items: our destination and our current location. Our current location is very important! Getting somewhere without knowing where you're starting from is impossible. There is no way to determine the right path without the right starting point.

On one occasion at my church, there was a revival service going on, standing room only. The worship leaders began to sing, ushering in the presence of God. Behind the scenes, some of the church leaders worried because the guest minister was delayed. When they contacted him, they discovered he was lost. One of the deacons began to direct him toward the church. Unfortunately, the deacon didn't know the minister's actual location. This delayed his arrival even longer, forcing the worship team to sing more hymns and songs. Finally, they found his correct location, and that minister arrived to deliver a powerful word.

Chapter 5: Knowing your Father

God gave Moses blueprints while he was on Mount Sinai for how to construct the tabernacle (Hebrews 8:5). This early temple was actually a copy of the real temple in heaven. It was divided into three distinct areas: the outer court, the inner court, and the holy of holies.

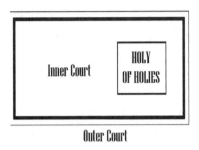

With God, nothing happens by accident. There is a purpose for everything, even these divisions in the temple. Under the Old Covenant, these three physical locations represented how close God's chosen people could move toward him, though this was not God's original purpose. Originally God's plan included the entire nation of Israel having unrestricted access to every area within the temple, including the holy of holies, the most intimate place. The people were to be his nation of priests (Exodus 19:5–6).

What happened? Eleven of the twelve tribes rejected this gift by deciding to build a golden calf for the purpose of worship while Moses was delayed on Mount Sinai (Exodus 32). God hates idolatry and pagan ritual. As a result, those eleven tribes forfeited the gift of being priests, leaving only the tribe of Levi to enter the temple beyond the outer court.

These three locations, although physical, can also represent our relationship with God. They can show us where we are and where we're going.

Outer Court

We all begin our journey in the outer court. This court was accessible to all, including the Levites (the priestly class), the high priest, the Jews, and the Gentiles. Basically,

Chapter 5: Knowing your Father

everyone was allowed to come into the outer court. The outer court was designed as a place for those whose access to worship and to God was restricted. But it became a place of counterfeit knowledge of God. Sacrificial animals were sold at a higher price than was honest, and moneychangers taxed individuals in the exchange of currency. The purpose of worship is not so men could profit financially but so they can profit spiritually. This is one reason why Jesus was so upset when he came into the temple and said, "My Father's House should be a House of Prayer but you have made it a den of thieves" (Matthew 21:13). The outer court had become intertwined with the world.

Likewise, many believers only know God in an outer court fashion. These outer court believers are saved by the precious blood of Jesus Christ the High Priest but are greatly influenced by the world. On the outside they attend worship services and do what good believers would. However, their hearts do not see or know the glory of the Lord (John 14:17).

Scripture gives us examples of those who have an outer court relationship with God. One that comes to mind is Ananias and Sapphira. In Acts 5, we find the story of Ananias and his wife, who decided to sell their possessions and give them to the church leaders to use in the Lord's work, as many believers at the time were doing. Although chapter 5 begins with the story of Ananias, the complete story actually begins in chapter 4. After seeing the praises Barnabas received from selling all his possessions and giving all he had to God and men, Ananias and his wife decided to follow Barnabas's example. However, they sold their property for one price, gave Peter a little less, and said they had given everything, like Barnabas—a rank lie. On the spot, God struck each of them down.

Giving is one of the main duties of a believer. However, giving is not always a good thing. Once, my cousin came to me extremely mad at her friends. I asked her what the problem was. She said, "They gave me this television." I thought, *Well, what's the problem? You have wanted a tele-*

Chapter 5: Knowing your Father

vision. Her friends had a yard sale, and everything they couldn't get rid of, they gave away. This television among them. It had some major problems. A videocassette was stuck in the player connected to it. It had no remote control, and the channel selection on the television did not work. She was frustrated because they had told her she was getting a great deal. Additionally, they had bragged about how they had blessed her! But in reality, they were merely trying to rid themselves of a burden and take credit where no credit was due.

On the outside everything looked okay, but their hearts told a different story. Much like Ananias and Sapphira, they had the wrong motivation for their giving. By contrast, Barnabas's reason for giving so much was not that he would receive praises from people. He just wanted to bless the kingdom of God. Something rooted deep within their spirits prevented Ananias and his wife from relinquishing all they had. This made them unable to press into the deeper things of God. They gave out of their surplus, but not out of their hearts. They wanted to be perceived in the same light as Barnabas, even if it meant deceiving God and men. However, it takes more than external actions to know God. God measures our relationship with him by our heart.

Jesus told the disciples a similar story in Mark 12:41–44. He compared the gold and silver of many rich people who gave to the temple in large amounts to a poor widow who gave two copper coins worth less than a penny. If you measured the gifts on a scale or placed them in a bank account, in every case the widow would have given least. But to Jesus, it was her heart that mattered. She gave all she had, whereas the rich people "gave out of their surplus," meaning what they could easily spare.

It's like that saying, "It's the thought that counts." When a child spends all day making a card for his father, it may have some misspellings, the cuts may be disproportionate, and much of the writing may even be unreadable. However, when the father sees this card, it is the most

Chapter 5: Knowing your Father

beautiful thing he has ever received. The father knows that not even Hallmark could duplicate this gift! He values the card in this way because the father knows the love the child put into it. He also knows the talent his child possesses. When the father adds all of these elements, it makes him value the card even more. This is how your heavenly Father is. In the parable of the poor widow, Jesus says, "They all gave out of their wealth; but she, out of her poverty, put in everything—all she had to live on" (Mark 12:44 NIV). The rich people in this story had an outer court relationship with the Father, much like Ananias. The widow is an example of someone who had more.

Not everyone who has an outer court relationship with God is like Ananias, Sapphira, or the rich people, satisfied with themselves and unwilling to go any farther. Many saints in the outer court are trapped in a man-made labyrinth. They long to please God but are confused. An invisible line has been drawn that says they can't cross. God did not create this line. This line is there because of the teachings they have received. They have limited their relationship with God based on man-made traditions. This man-made labyrinth makes it impossible to press into the deeper things of God. It stunts the growth of many. However, the time is coming when God will allow this no longer. The labyrinth must come down!

Long ago, there was a nation of people whom God loved. They were not Jews, but they were chosen.

They were stuck in a labyrinth, but their hearts wanted to please God. This nation of people was so confused that they didn't know that they didn't know their right hand from their left (Jonah 4:11). Their spiritual discernment was off. Their actions expressed confusion. But in their hearts was a desire to please God. Of course, it was God who had placed it there (Ecclesiastes 3:11). In fact, this desire is placed in the hearts of all men, but only a few yield to it, even after hearing the Word (Romans 1:19–22). In this case, God sent Jonah to confirm his Word and the desire placed in their hearts. Once the Word was preached

Chapter 5: Knowing your Father

and they understood what God truly wanted from them, the people of Nineveh repented.

Many of us today are no better than Nineveh or the lame man who asked Peter for a few dimes (Acts 3:6). God through Peter had more to offer, and he gave this man the power to walk and run again.

I can relate to Nineveh and the lame man because my life is a mirror of theirs. I was a Christian, but something was missing. My spiritual senses were dulled. My vision was blurred. I could neither taste the goodness of God (Psalm 34:8) nor touch his fully extended hand (Isaiah 59:1). Part of my inability to do these things was because people had taught me it was impossible or that I did not qualify. Then there were times in my life when I didn't try or know where to begin. The traditions of man had placed a sense of ineligibility upon me. Then a revelation came to me, and suddenly the door blew open. So if you're in this place, don't feel discouraged! Many believers who have gone into a deeper relationship with God have also been here.

The young Samuel ministered before the Lord, yet he had an outer court relationship with the Father and nothing more. However, late one night God began to call him to a deeper relationship with him, just like he is calling all of us (1 Samuel 3). The next level is an inner court relationship.

Inner Court

We were late for the game. As we entered the arena, our anticipation only grew. We were celebrating my brother's birthday, watching the Sixers vs. the Heat. The groans of the crowd let us know the home team (Philadelphia 76ers) must be losing. We had to slow down because of the congestion of fans headed in the same direction. As we approached the gate, we were given a white towel representing the home team. Fans were decked out in their team gear. The colors red, white, and blue filled the arena. Unsure of where to go, we located an usher. After looking

Chapter 5: Knowing your Father

at our ticket stubs, he pointed all the way to the top of the stadium. When we finally made it to the top, the first quarter was nearly over and we were losing by seventeen points. We sat so close to the ceiling that if we had moved three more rows back, we could have touched it. It was a packed arena that night as the number-one team in the league was in town: the Miami Heat.

With the game already a blowout, my attention turned elsewhere. As I scanned the crowd, I saw the private box seating. This was a special seating area. Those with access to it were living it up. There were waiters, fine dining, and a large flat-screen television. You name it, they had it. They were able to have access and enjoy pleasures that I could only dream about. But of course, they had paid much more for their tickets than I had.

Enjoying the finer things in life and having access to special places will cost you. In the temple of God, there was a special area known as the Inner court or the holy place. Only the high priest and Levites were allowed to enter into the holy place. It was off-limits to everyone else. Priests entered into this part of the temple every morning and every evening, offering morning incense and evening incense. These represented prayer, worship, and communion with God.

Yet in the inner court, God still measures our relationship with him by our hearts. In 1 Samuel, Eli and his sons had the honor of accessing the inner court since they were Levites and Eli the high priest. Having access to the inner court was their birthright. However, Eli and his sons took it for granted. They were very wicked and did not fear the Lord (1 Samuel 2:21). Scripture says, "The fear of the Lord is the beginning of wisdom" (Proverbs 9:10 NIV). You can tell Eli's lack of reverence and fear of the Lord by his reaction to the words Samuel said concerning his coming death. Eli simply responded by saying, "He is the LORD; let him do what is good in his eyes" (1 Samuel 2:12 NIV). No repentance, no fear, very nonchalant.

What steps does it take to move beyond an outer court

Chapter 5: Knowing your Father

and toward an inner court relationship with God? If you want to have this type of access, it's going to cost you. But it is worth the price.

The good news is there are only a few steps required. The bad news is these steps are immeasurable—and actually, that may also be good news. Each of us holds a special place in the heart of God. This means that the steps I take to the holy place may not necessarily take you there. However, one element is required for all to enter in. David writes in Psalm 24:4, "Who shall ascend into the hill of the LORD? Or who shall stand in his holy place? He that hath clean hands, and a pure heart; who hath not lifted up his soul unto vanity, nor sworn deceitfully" (KJV). In Acts 5, Ananias and his wife swore deceitfulness in their hearts from the start. They held back with their hands. This led to them lifting up their souls to vanity. A pure heart is essential to entering the holy place.

Individuals like David may confuse this issue for some people. David is known as a man after God's own heart. But he was guilty of coveting—stealing another man's wife—and not honoring his father and mother by this behavior. David broke nearly half of the commandments in his adultery with Bathsheba and then his murder of her husband. David had the right heart, but at that time he committed many sins, which God eventually forgave.

Once my sister was reading the Bible, and she said, "What is David doing in the Bible? I thought everyone in there was perfect."

All of us search for a person with perfect actions. When we look around, we see there are none—"For all have sinned and fall short of the glory of God" (Romans 3:23, NIV). In a sense, no person ever born will possess a clean slate. This is when we must look inward, to the holy place, because that is where God looks.

In Psalm 51, we can see what God saw in David. We can see the invisible.

Despite our outward actions, God still searches the heart of men. In David's case, he found a heart that truly

Chapter 5: Knowing your Father

desired relationship with him above all things. The same is true with us; our actions don't necessarily reflect what is in our hearts. This is one reason why we must judge ourselves, our own hearts. We need only to pray and let your Father deal with those who reflect His image, no matter how distorted they appear.

However, our hands do tell a truth. Our "hands" in Psalm 24 are related to our outward actions. We clean, type, steal, kill, bless, and curse with our hands. Both the beauties of life and the pain of death flow through our hands. The key word is *flow*. Where do our actions flow from? What is the source? Scripture says that out of the abundance of the heart, the mouth speaks (Luke 6:45). A similar statement can be made about our hands: out of the abundance of the heart the hands do. Cain killed Abel with his hands because of the jealousy in his heart. Abel made an acceptable sacrifice because of his desire to please God (Genesis 4:4).

What is your heart conceiving through your hands? This is what Jesus meant in Matthew 5:28 when he said, "But I tell you that anyone who looks at a woman lustfully has already committed adultery with her in his heart" (NIV). Only God truly knows your heart. As you seek him, he will purify your heart through forgiveness and growth. A pure heart and clean hands lead to the inner court.

There is one Pharisee mentioned in the Bible who was able to enter the inner court. He was a very humble man who feared the Lord. We know him by the name of Nicodemus. He was a member of the Sanhedrin, the ruling body in Israel, and a highly respected teacher of the Old Testament Scriptures. Because of a conversation he had with Jesus, recorded in John 3, all who hear his questions and Jesus' words are able to learn the way of salvation.

Nicodemus desired more than salvation. What I mean by this statement is that he wasn't satisfied with merely accepting Christ. He wanted more than an outer court relationship. We know this by his actions, because he met

Chapter 5: Knowing your Father

with Jesus at peculiar times. He sacrificed sleep to meet with him early in the morning and late at night. It wasn't a facade for Nicodemus; he pursued God, and he did it continually (John 7:50–51). He didn't let his peers, his position, lack of sleep, or man's traditions deter him. If you want an Inner court relationship with God, you must continually seek him. We can be tricked into thinking we have arrived after being consistent for a couple of weeks. It is a daily pursuit. We must continually find a way to make time to fellowship with the Father.

Holy of Holies

Finally we come to the holy of holies, also referred to as the most holy place. This is where all of us should desire to be. In the tabernacle, a veil separated the holy place and the most holy place. No ordinary person could go beyond the veil and enter this sacred room. Only the high priest was allowed to enter into this place, and that was only once a year on the Day of Atonement for the purpose of making a sin offering for the whole nation of Israel so they could be forgiven.

In the holy of holies, God would manifest himself. He would appear as a pillar of cloud and fire. The very presence and power of God were present within the holy of holies. In the Old Testament, Aaron, Zechariah, and Zadok were just a few high priests who were able to enter the most holy place.

A very thick veil separated the holy of holies from the inner court. This veil had a very special design that sent a message to everyone who looked on it. An embroidered cherub (a heavenly creature) on the veil served as a symbol to sinful men that they were unable to enter into the holy of holies. This creature reminded them of the angel with the flaming sword that guarded the way to the tree of life (Genesis 3:24).

Unlike Eden, the high priest could enter into this place after the sprinkling of the blood sacrifice at the altar (Hebrews 9:7). Scripture says only a high priest can enter

Chapter 5: Knowing your Father

the holy of holies. Yet there are many who entered the real most holy place. Abraham, Paul, David, Moses, John the apostle, and Daniel all entered it. These mighty saints went through the veil and entered the most holy place of God. What makes this conversation more interesting is *how* they entered the most holy place. In some instances the most holy place of the tabernacle or temple was yet to be built or had been destroyed. In each case, none of the men qualified to enter the most holy place, since none were high priests. So how were they able to enter the most holy place?

If we think of the true holy of holies as a geographical location, we will never go beyond the veil. The most holy place has no borders. It is in heaven yet on earth. It can be in the restroom of a football stadium or a chapel in the Appalachian Mountains. Paul went to the holy of holies in the desert of Arabia. The apostle John encountered it on Patmos Island. Daniel was able to abide in the most holy place while living in Babylon. Abraham experienced it in a country he did not know. King David was able to go beyond the veil continuously without any animal sacrifice. What I'm speaking of is not a physical location.

All these great men knew a secret that Jesus would reveal to his disciples concerning communion with God in the holy of holies. King David even wrote about it in Psalm 91: "He that dwells in the secret place of the Most High, shall abide in the shadow of the almighty." The secret place is another name for the holy of holies. The secret of communion with God has nothing to do with a geographical location, nor do you need a special title to access it. The holy of holies is within you, as Jesus said in Luke 17:21: "The kingdom of God is within you" (NIV).

What does this mean? This statement of Jesus' is one of the more mysterious Scriptures. It means to recognize the divine that is within you. Jesus desires us to understand that in a way, the finite contains the infinite. It's comparable to believing you can fit all the waters of the earth in a sixteen-ounce glass. God is infinitely immeasurable. Yet

Chapter 5: Knowing your Father

He is within us (1 John 4:4). I am perplexed in trying to express what this means with mere words. Theologians have spent lifetimes defining this truth. But as Jesus has told us to do, let's ponder this truth through the eyes of a child.

Lessons from Cartoons

When I was a child, I enjoyed watching the cartoon *Popeye*. Popeye was just an ordinary sailor until he consumed a can of spinach. Once the spinach entered into his system, he became extraordinary. He could lift cars, walk through walls, and most importantly save his girlfriend, Olive. No obstacle was able to overtake or hinder him, including the strong man, Brutus. From a scientific perspective, spinach is incapable of causing such a transformation. As a child I didn't care whether this was possible; it only amazed me. It even encouraged me to eat spinach!

Similarly, as we look at entering into God's presence, let's not become bogged down in the how. Instead, let's place our energy on entering into the most holy place. Three keys to entering into the most holy place are prayer, worship, and sometimes fasting.

We will talk about prayer and fasting in their own chapters, so for now, let's focus on worship. I remember as a child, worship was nothing more than an exercise session for me. But as I examined Scripture, I embraced the power of worship. Worship was so powerful that Jehoshaphat appointed singers to lead Israel into battle (2 Chronicles 20:21). Acts 16:23–26 tells of a worship service in prison. Paul and Silas sang praises to God in prison, and suddenly a great earthquake came.

The prison doors opened, and they were loosed of their chains. When you worship God, the power of God manifests and breaks through. It opens a spiritual window or door. When you worship, you allow God to intervene on your behalf. I have witnessed that when the church is truly worshiping God, the Spirit is loosed.

Even the delivery of the written and prophetic Word

Chapter 5: Knowing your Father

becomes like a skilled surgeon performing laser surgery on his patients. I'm so excited about this, I think I will worship right now! Keep in mind, our heavenly Father is not concerned about what our worship sounds like in the natural. He is looking for the heart that is beyond the voice. I'm not saying this just because I have no singing talent whatsoever. When you worship, God (your Heavenly Father) will move and bring you into the most holy place. When we reach this place, God may give us the power to overcome the strongman, who is our enemy: the Devil and all of his devices.

In the physical temple, most people were barred from accessing the holy of holies. Today, it is different. The way is open for us all because of the work of Jesus. Your heavenly Father tore the veil from top to bottom (Luke 23:45). The significance of his tearing the veil is that his desire to be with us is greater than our desire to be with him. A title will never give you access to the most holy place.

Only he can, and he already has. You simply need to realize it and press in. This is where we can learn from those who practice Gnosticism. The Greek word for *Gnostic* means "to know," but it does not refer to academic or scientific knowledge. It speaks of a self-knowledge or awareness of the Spirit of God within you. When you realize this and walk through the torn veil, you will have true communion with the Father (Matthew 6:11). You will realize that He is more than the titles or attributes you place on Him. He is more than just God, the man upstairs, Yah, I Am, and the Creator of all, Elohim. But He is your heavenly Father, not just mine or those who attend a building on certain days.

CHAPTER 6
KNOWING THE SECRET PLACE

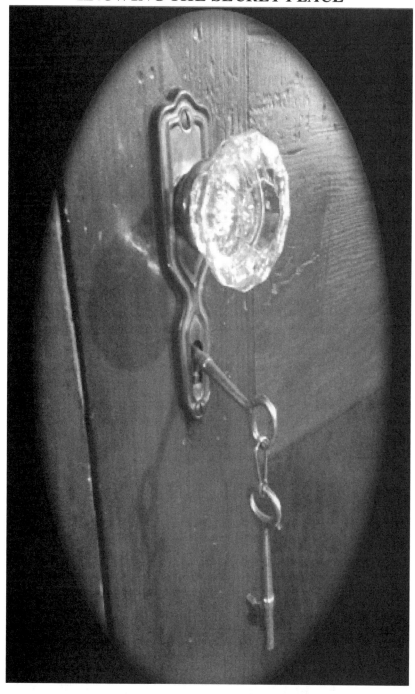

Chapter 6: Knowing the Secret Place

It was Christmas break, and four of my college friends and I planned to attend a Christian college conference in Atlanta. The plan was to meet in O'Fallon to board a bus at 10:00 a.m., about thirty-five minutes outside of Saint Louis right off Interstate 64. The day finally arrived. We drove from Kansas City, headed east across Interstate 70. We arrived earlier than anticipated due to our speedy driving. We sat around in the hotel parking lot until 10:00 a.m., but the bus wasn't there. After about twenty-five minutes, we decided to call Brian from the hotel and see what the delay was. He picked up the cell, and we asked when we should see him. He responded, "We are already here waiting on you!"

After roughly a ten-minute conversation, we discovered that we were in the right city but the wrong state! We were in O'Fallon, Missouri, which is about thirty-five minutes west of Saint Louis. We were supposed to be in O'Fallon, Illinois, about thirty-five minutes east of Saint Louis. We ended up missing the bus due to being in the wrong place. On that day, we thought we were in the right place—right state, right city, and right building—until someone told us otherwise. Similarly, life can present you with a mirage. You might think you're in the right place, but when the truth is presented, you'll discover something very different.

The Secret Place

Jesus spoke of a group of individuals who appeared to be in the secret place of communion with God. From the outside, they were in the right place: saying the right words, wearing the right clothing, and even holding the right titles. But Jesus said not to be like them because they had no idea what it truly meant to stand before the presence of God in the secret place. The secret place, the holy of holies, is sacred. Many have a desire to be in this place, but Jesus says there is only one way to get there. In Matthew 6, Jesus gives us one of the most famous prayers in the world: the Lord's Prayer. However, before giving it,

Chapter 6: Knowing the Secret Place

he offers a game plan for what to do before we pray. This plan is comparable to planning a home-cooked meal.

When I first began to cook, I remember skipping directly to the part where you add the ingredients—two eggs, butter, and milk—to the cake or whatever you're making. But for most recipes, there is a part you need to do before you mix things together. Those are the preparation stages, where you set the temperature of the oven, let the food thaw, etc. When you don't follow all of the directions, your plan can result in a host of problems—the food might not be as tasty, might not be prepared correctly, or might not be ready on time.

This is also true with prayer and communion with God. You cannot just rush into prayer without preparation, especially in the earlier stages of learning how to pray. Jesus informed us what we must do as we prepare to pray. He said when you pray, go into your room, close the door, and pray to your Father who is unseen.

Tameion: The Storeroom

Here we find three steps to entering the secret place: 1. go into a room, 2. close the door, and 3. pray to your Father. I have done this countless times—gone into a room, closed the door, and prayed to the Father—with no results. It's easier said than done. Sometimes I think I'm doing so well: I'm in the room, the door is closed . . . but suddenly the bills start to speak, the car problems come, my son knocks on the door, there's a phone ringing, birds are chirping, the air blows, you name it. Besides the three obvious steps, what is Jesus truly saying to us about prayer? Let's examine the first step: going into a room. The Greek word for "room" here is *tameion*. The tameion was actually a specific type of room. There are many rooms in a house—bedroom, kitchen, office, front room—and each has its specific purpose (though sometimes my bedroom is turned into the dining room and the front room into the bedroom for various reasons).

Chapter 6: Knowing the Secret Place

But what is the tameion, and what is its purpose? The same word is used by Jesus in Luke 12:24 when he says, "Consider the ravens, they do not sow or reap, they have no storeroom [tameion]; yet God feeds them. And how much more valuable you are than birds" (NIV).

The tameion is a place of storage, a place of extra, a place beyond measure. Did you read that? The tameion is a room that is beyond measure, beyond numbering, beyond counting, and beyond what your mind can comprehend (1 Corinthians 2:9).

One of my favorite stories that references storerooms is the one recorded in Genesis 41. In this story, Pharaoh had a dream of seven fat cows and seven skinny cows that not only perplexed him but also remained inscrutable to all of his wise men. Not one was able to understand or interpret it. Then the chief cupbearer remembered one of his old cell buddies who had a gift to interpret dreams: a young Hebrew slave named Joseph.

Pharaoh sent for Joseph from the dungeon and explained the dream. Then Joseph, with the help of the Holy Spirit, told him the meaning: famine was coming upon the land, and he needed to make preparations. As a result of this interpretation, Pharaoh appointed Joseph as the second-highest person in all of Egypt. His task was to prepare Egypt for this famine. Joseph, with the anointing of the Holy Spirit, was able to accumulate so much that in Genesis 41:49 it says they had to stop keeping records because they had so much surplus in the storeroom. Some versions say it was beyond measure. Like Joseph, we have a storeroom we can access that is beyond measure. However, unlike Joseph, it is not our responsibility to stock this storeroom but only to commune with our Father, who is the filler of the storeroom.

Look at what it says in Ephesians 3:14–20:

For this reason I kneel before the Father, from whom every family in heaven and on earth derives its name. I pray that out of his glorious riches he may strengthen

Chapter 6: Knowing the Secret Place

you with power through his Spirit in your inner being, so that Christ may dwell in your hearts through faith. And I pray that you, being rooted and established in love, may have power, together with all the Lord's holy people, to grasp how wide and long and high and deep is the love of Christ, and to know this love that surpasses knowledge—that you may be filled to the measure of all the fullness of God. Now to him who is able to do immeasurably more than all we ask or imagine, according to his power that is at work within us.

What then is in this spiritual tameion for us? Our storeroom contains health, spiritual gifts, revelation, comfort, joy, peace, direction, manifestations, and something that Paul called "immeasurably more." Though every godly need, want, and desire is available in the storeroom, the manifestation of it all depends on what you allow to work within you. If you're in the secret place and you're like me and look around and you see books, unfolded clothes, a window, and a bed to sleep on while you're attempting to commune with God, then that is all you will have working within you. That means you need to work on the next step, which is closing the door.

Learning to Focus: Math 101

It was my first week in trigonometry. None of my friends had made it to this level of math. In my other classes, I always had a few friends to keep me company. Usually we had assigned seats. In this class, it was a free-for-all. The shape of the class and other features were factors in determining seating. Since there were no windows, it seemed like most students sat toward the middle or back. This happened because they didn't want to be too close to the instructor, but they also didn't want to be too far.

My selection of my seat was strategic. Sitting in the front of class right next to the door would help me stay in contact with friends. Occasionally, my friends would

Chapter 6: Knowing the Secret Place

roam the hall. So I would have access to communicate with them from my location. The teacher of this course was an older gentleman who surely wouldn't notice. Most of my teachers only wanted to survive until the next day. The previous semester, I'd had a teacher who we nicknamed Ms. Hennessy. Instead of coffee in her cup, she would bring an alcoholic drink.

Maybe it was to calm her nerves from her work environment. Some of my classmates would often leave her class unnoticed. My expectation for this trig class was no different. After all, I had never heard of this guy.

The first week, like all first weeks, seemed long. This teacher appeared pretty clever too. Friday was the end of the week. My teacher wrote some very important notes on the board. A shadowy image in the hallway caught my attention. Just as I had anticipated, my friends were there, begging me to leave the class.

From my body language, my friends knew they would have to work extra hard to get me out of my seat. The instructor continued writing notes on the board with his back toward the class. I inched closer to the door. Suddenly, he slammed the door shut. He then turned to the class and said, "I will not allow any distractions in this classroom." Additionally, he said, "What goes on out there is none of your concern. You only need to focus on what is taking place in here."

In the same way, when we enter the secret place, we should be focused. We must close the door. Closing the door on external interferences is the easy part. But closing the door of the mind, the spiritual door, is more challenging. After all, it is the issues of life that bring us into the secret place to begin with. The worries, the problems, the concerns, they all drive us to this room. So why should we close the door on these issues? It's not that we close the door on our problems. But we close the door on the position they currently have in our lives.

There is a famous statement that says, "Don't tell God how big your problems are, but tell your problems how

Chapter 6: Knowing the Secret Place

big your God is." The point of this statement is that our problems are nothing in comparison to God. Once we are in the secret place, the goal is to lay our problems down (1 Peter 5:7). When we release the problems, the worries, and the concerns, then we make room for what God has to offer.

Closing the door places your problems in their proper position—under your feet. Additionally, it causes you to focus on what your heavenly Father desires to give and teach you. That is why my trig instructor closed the door. We needed to prepare for the test, to stay focused on what he wanted us to learn.

In the book of 2 Kings 4:33, we see Elisha shutting the door as he prayed for the widow's dead son. His intention in closing the door was to focus on the problem of the dead boy. He didn't want the death that was on the outside interfering with the life on the inside. This allowed him to focus.

We have all come across the problem of praying with a racing mind. Thinking about what we will eat or drink, or how long we have been in this room. If you cannot control your mind, you will not be able to complete the second step of closing the door.

One of the best methods I have heard for closing the door or controlling your mind can be compared to flying a kite. Flying a kite is not difficult, although it can be if not done correctly. In order to fly a kite, you need the right conditions: a breezy day and a place free of wires or trees. When controlling your mind, the wind represents thoughts that bombard our minds during prayer. Most of the time we go with our thoughts, resulting in us losing our minds with the wind. When this happens, you let the wind take the kite wherever it pleases. The wind will not care if your kite ends up stuck in a tree or some cabling. Sometimes it will even break your kite, rendering it useless.

The kite represents the mind. We have the ability to harness our thoughts during prayer like a kite flier

Chapter 6: Knowing the Secret Place

harnessing a kite. We don't have to be moved by every thought. We must control and guard our thoughts and hearts during this time in the secret place, as Proverbs 4:23 says: "Above all else, guard your heart, for everything you do flows from it" (NIV).

If you're able to control your mind, you will become aware of what God is doing. This is something I have experienced in my own life. If we give God time to work with us, he will.

It was a Wednesday like every other Wednesday. I was in my usual place toward the back of the sanctuary with the sound equipment as I meditated. My attention gradually was drawn to what was before my eyes. I stood there watching them play. It was as though I had seen this scene before, but I had not. They hit the volleyball back and forth over the net. For some reason, I had a desire to join them. Without me saying a word, one of the individuals walked over to me. My excitement grew, as I hoped he would ask me to join them. He told me, "The reason we are playing volleyball is because no one is praying. Our hands are tied, and we can do nothing. Our desire is to work in communion with you and God." Then it dawned on me that these individuals I was watching were ministering angels. As soon as I came to this realization, the scene quickly faded. There I was, standing in my usual place at Wednesday prayer.

The angels had faded away. Only two praying saints were in view among the many empty seats.

Like angels, Satan and his minions are also very active during our times of prayer. They have a very unorthodox strategy that has worked time and time again: they make their thoughts our thoughts (2 Corinthians 11:3). Eve ate the fruit because Satan sold her an idea. It's like watching a commercial where an advertiser says, "This item will make a difference in your life." Then you go to the store quoting what you heard on television as if it was your idea. They have made their thoughts your thoughts. Often we don't need what those advertisers are selling us. We

Chapter 6: Knowing the Secret Place

definitely don't need what the Devil is telling us!

We must refuse those thoughts, like Paul says in 2 Corinthians 10:5: "We demolish arguments and every pretension that sets itself up against the knowledge of God, and we take captive every thought to make it obedient to Christ" (NIV).

Prayer is a time for communing with God. However, sometimes conflict is unavoidable, even in the secret place. God desires that we argue, disagree, and wage spiritual warfare with Satan during prayer. This is so we can remain in the secret place. Spiritual warfare is an important piece of closing the door.

Just My Imagination

There was no need for a clock in this dimension. Nor was there progress to goodness, since everything was more than perfect. In him dwelt abundant life, and he was surrounded by it as well. He imagined a new world, a different place. It would be filled with great wonders. What he envisioned was grand.

As he continued to visualize, he saw great stars of light that reflected his goodness and mercy. In his mind, he envisioned spheres of different sizes and elements. Each one would reflect a different aspect of his nature. Then he imagined one sphere that was special. Much imagination went into the framing of this place. He perceived oceans, seas, land, and plants, and this was only the beginning. Animals of the air, creeping things from the ground, and many creatures in between were suspended in his mind. However, the best was yet to be imagined. He imagined creatures that would be made just like him, in his likeness and image.

All of this was imagined before the first tick of the clock, according to Scripture. In Hebrews 11:3, it says, "By faith we understand that the worlds were framed by the word of God" (NIV). What is interesting here is the Hebrew word for "frame," which is *yetzer*. When you translate this word literally, you get the English word *imagination*. So

Chapter 6: Knowing the Secret Place

why is it translated "frame" in most of our translations? The ancient Hebrews and even Greeks believed there were two aspects of the mind. The first aspect is the analytical mind. This is the thought and reasoning part of the mind. The Greek word for this is *nous*, which is used in Scripture: "Then opened he their understanding [nous], that they might understand the scriptures" (Luke 24:45).

The second aspect of the mind is where creativity and imagination dwell, and that's where the word *yetzer* comes in. Neither aspect of the mind is greater than the other, but they both work with one accord. Before God said "Let there be," the whole of creation was already in his mind (yetzer).

The question is, how does this apply to me? How can I make this wisdom relevant in my life and manifest my destiny? Let's analyze a few other times the Bible uses this terminology. In Genesis 6:5, it says, "The LORD saw how great man's wickedness on the earth had become, and that every inclination of the thoughts of his heart was only evil all the time" (NIV). Again, we find the word *yetzer* behind the word *inclination*. These people were not only judged on what they had become but because of what was yet to come. To God, imagination is a very powerful tool. After all, it is how the worlds were framed! The yetzer represents the unseen, the invisible, the spiritual, the future, that which hasn't manifested yet. So God foresaw more evil was coming.

We all have opportunity to use our imaginations for something great. The imagination is not only a tool for evil. Nor is it only so we can imagine how many NBA championships we could have won if we'd had a chance or indulge in wishful thinking. It serves a greater spiritual purpose. Isaiah 26:3 says, "He will keep us in perfect peace whose mind [yetzer] is continually stayed on him" (NIV). We all desire peace, so let's imagine thoughts of God.

There is a battle waging for our imaginations. There are several battlefronts all circulating from the source of Satan. One of those fronts is television. My wife says tele-

Chapter 6: Knowing the Secret Place

vision is basically someone "telling you a vision." When you dissect the word *television*, it means to see from a distance. What we see and are told, though from a distance, helps frame our yetzer. Much of what we view is not necessarily bad. True, there is a lot of trash on television, but not everything falls into that category. What I want to focus on here is how TV affects you, even if it's good, fun entertainment like a sports show or a cartoon. No matter what you're watching, it can hinder your mind from receiving from God. Personally, I find watching television to be a good break from time to time. However, we cannot let it consume us. According to Neilsen, people spend an average of six hours a day watching television. That is nearly one-third of the day. For most of us, the rest of our time is spent sleeping and working. That does not leave much space for God to operate!

With that in mind, we must not become consumed by TV. Even Christian programs can do this to us. They hypnotize us by trapping us on the couch, doing nothing and thinking nothing. Many great inventions, businesses, and ideas never leave the couch. In fact, some of these ideas are not even allowed to develop in our minds because of various media. Our minds become filled with sitcoms and television shows, leaving no room to develop from within. Our imaginations are already occupied.

A Child's Imagination

Maybe we can learn from our childhood in this respect. When I was a child, my imagination entertained me for hours. In childhood, my bed was a spaceship traveling to the other side of the universe. The backyard was a combat zone. We all have those memories. But life happened, the bills called, and imagination took on a different role.

In my mature years, my imagination is more tamed. I am no longer in a distant galaxy far away but imagining what it would be like to get off work early or daydreaming about some other task that needs to be accomplished. There is nothing wrong with this, since you may run into

Chapter 6: Knowing the Secret Place

many solutions through such imagining! But you don't have to limit yourself to just that.

You are made in the image of your Father. My son walks exactly like me. I didn't teach him; it just came naturally to him. The same is true with you. There are some aspects of us that just are natural, or in our case, supernatural. Imagination is one of them. So find a story in the Bible. Not just any story but a story that is special to you. It could be when the raven fed the prophet or when Jesus called Lazarus out of death. How about Peter healing with his shadow? It could be Jesus seeking the Father early in the morning. Whatever it is, take that story.

Use your imagination in the secret place. Imagine filling out a resume and being hired. Visualize healing the sick. Perceive the defeat of your mental issues. Don't neglect this wisdom! Don't become stuck on terms like *visualize* and *perceive*, saying they are New Age terms when in fact they are valid spiritual tools that the church has not really taken advantage of. Don't take your imagination for granted. This is part of what Paul refers to when he says, "I pray that the eyes of your heart will be enlightened" (Ephesians 1:18 NIV). Everything God has to offer is within you; now run with it. We all know how to imagine. Just do what you have always done. This time, however, do it with intent, knowing you are framing the purpose of God!

One-on-One with Your Father

It was Sunday morning, and we were off to church for a prayer meeting. My mother and I were frequent churchgoers; however, this time, two of my nephews had come along. When we arrived in the parking lot, my mother explained to my nephews that we would be praying to God. One of my nephews, who must have been nine at the time, asked a marvelous question. The words came off his lips with great excitement and expectation: "So we are going to speak with God, and God is going to speak to us?" My mother and I both smiled. My smile was one

Chapter 6: Knowing the Secret Place

of amazement. *I can't believe he asked that question. Why didn't I think to ask that question?* Would God really speak, I wondered? Maybe he would. "Of course he will," my mother said.

When we walked into the church, everyone was in a position of prayer. Some were walking around, others were on bended knee, and some were sitting in rocking chairs. The space heaters in the front and back of the sanctuary seemed to have no effect. It was so cold you could see your breath as you prayed.

We found our seats and began to pray. My nephews, still unsure of what to do, mostly listened and watched. The one who had asked the questions was hoping to hear from God. When prayer service ended, we said our goodbyes to the other prayer warriors. As we drove down the road on our way home, my nephew asked, "Did God speak?" My mother said yes. But I found myself wondering if that was true. Had I been communing with the Father? When I was a child, I too hoped to hear God's voice. But as I grew older, that hope left my mind. Maybe prayer was only meant to be a one-way road. But I didn't really believe that, did I? For many years I had witnessed ministers of God who said they possessed the power to hear God speak. These individuals revealed information and revelation that would be impossible for them to know on their own. There was no doubt in my mind they had communed with God. Then it became clear to me. I had never doubted God could speak. But I wondered why he never spoke to me. Maybe I wasn't special enough.

One-Way Communication

For years, prayer for me was only a time to voice my concerns to my heavenly Father. My only preparation for prayer was making sure I had my wish list together. This list included names of individuals to pray for and decisions I needed clarity on. In hindsight, this was a very religious practice. My heart was in the right place. But this is not a complete picture of prayer. I left no chance

Chapter 6: Knowing the Secret Place

for God to respond and give me direction. Yet, like my nephew, I eagerly desired to hear from God.

It was about five years later when I began to verbalize my desire to hear God speak. My desire was not to be a prophet who possesses inner knowledge to give to others; I only needed direction and confirmation for issues I faced. Sounds selfish in a way, but I knew I was unable to provide direction for others when I was still confused. My mind was full of doubt as to whether God would speak to me. Many questions arose from within. Why do I need to hear God speak? Aren't the written oracles of God enough? Why would God want to speak to me? I have never lived in a monastery or gone overseas for mission work. What would qualify me to hear from God?

My desire was to be just as in tune with God as those ministers who would visit for revival. On occasion I would ask these men how they heard from God. One prophet instructed me to read the Word. This was something I already did. But my results were not the same as his. Many others said it was a gift and only certain people had this ability. My spirit was not in agreement with this answer. Then one day, I was listening to a minister on television. He said anyone could hear from God. You just need to know you can. The minister added that you have to make the truths of the Bible *your* truths, meaning you have to make them real to you. Suddenly, in my spirit, what seemed like an invisible barrier began to break. I began to tell people the promises and revelation God was giving me. Yet it seemed like many others had an invisible barrier too. It wasn't just me. The fact was, what I was saying and aspiring to do was against traditions created by men.

A Spiritual Caste System

There is no way someone who does not hold the position of a prophet can hear from God in such a way. Maybe I'm wrong for aspiring to hear from God. These were thoughts I struggled with at the beginning. I had to press through what appeared to be a spiritual separation. I began to

Chapter 6: Knowing the Secret Place

notice that in the church, there were those who had and those who lacked. You could go no further than your current spiritual position or title.

This separation is comparable to the ancient Indian caste system. In this system, people were divided into five castes. Brahmans were the highest class. Those in this class were the educated—writers, thinkers, and religious workers. Kshatriyas ranked second, holding positions as rulers, property owners, and warriors who protected the boundaries of the country. Then there were the Vaishyas, who were skilled traders, merchants, and minor officials. Next there were the Shudras, who were to assist the other castes. They were unskilled laborers. Last were the Untouchables. They lived lives of discrimination and poverty and were considered outsiders in their own land.

Some say the original intent of the system was to produce order. However, as time passed, the system became an organized discrimination machine. Whatever caste you were born into, that would forever be your destiny. You were unable to marry anyone of a different caste or else you faced criminal charges. Additionally, people of lower castes were restricted to separate drinking fountains, separate places of worship, and even eating separately. The defining lines in this caste system were invisible to the outsider or the one who was undiscerning. (This system has been officially eliminated through legislation, though there are still remnants of it in the country.)

India is not unique in this. All countries and cultures have experienced and are experiencing such systems. Sadly, such a system also exists in the church. There are basically two main branches of the church: clergy and laymen. Laymen have a variety of responsibilities. They write newsletters, serve as ushers, set up sound equipment, clean toilets, and carry out various other duties. On the other hand, clergy minister the Word, counsel, and pray. At first glance, nothing is wrong with this system. But we need to look deeper. The church was designed to be a community of great influence. The church should be

Chapter 6: Knowing the Secret Place

a place of leaders, not followers; a place of servants, not a place of greed or of one above all.

It should be a place of restoration instead of a place of condemnation. It has become a place of red-tape bureaucracy, often failing to connect with individuals. The hearts of men, just like in the Indian caste system, have corrupted the original intent. In many denominations, clergy have become superstars. They are treated like kings: surrounded by bodyguards, pampered, and highly esteemed. While some clergy manage to receive such treatment with a servant's heart, holding these clergy in such high esteem while devaluing others handicaps and limits the laymen and even Jesus.

Laymen—regular church members—travel from church to church, revival to revival, and conference to conference. They desire to receive a word, a healing, or some other type of blessing from the clergy. Most clergy are humble and try to minister to as many as possible. I spoke to one pastor the other day. He spoke of how overwhelmed he was from the hospital and home visits. Then there was the counseling of others till the early hours in the morning. Often he was left with nothing to look forward to but repeating the process the following day. At one point, he found himself in the hospital from the stress of the position!

If only laymen realized their own potential! Imagine the heartache you could save your pastor. Clergy are incapable of giving everyone else what they desire and need, though they may want to. This handicap must be removed.

We must remember that the veil has been torn. God's call to all of his children today is no different than it was originally. All of us are called to ministry (Ephesians 4:11), we all possess a spiritual gift (1 Corinthians 12), and God desires for all of us to move beyond the veil. But not knowing we have this access, many laymen have become nothing more than pew warmers. We wait for the clergy to give us the Word of God. This is comparable to a mother feeding a baby off her plate. Why are we settling

Chapter 6: Knowing the Secret Place

for crumbs as children of God? We as laymen discriminate against ourselves, believing only clergy possess the ability to provide deliverance or hear from God. If you allow God to do it, he will use you as an apostle in the janitors' break room, as a prophet in the lecture hall, as an evangelist within the walls of the church, as the pastor of your family and extended family, as the teacher among those holding PhDs.

We don't realize we can go to the king for ourselves. We have the same access as the woman with the issue of the blood (Luke 8). Yes, true: sometimes we need a prophet or a minister to take us because we don't know the way (Romans 10:14). But Jesus' desire is for us to go to God for ourselves. Jesus himself says in John 16:26, "In that day you will ask in my name. I am not saying that I will ask the Father on your behalf" (NIV). You can be the best video editor, janitor, or usher in the world and at the same time heal the sick, preach a word, win the lost, and bring salvation and all of its manifestations.

Don't limit what God desires to do through you! Don't box yourself in the traditions of men. Realize that God has created you to be part of a royal priesthood (2 Peter 1:3). You possess more than an ability to hold a smile on your face or to bake the best pie anyone could ever imagine.

Hearing beyond the Wind

Clergy were never meant to do all the work of the church. We are all individual beings, but we must work together as the body of Christ. There is a specific work for each of us. God gives us direction through the Word, and hearing him through the Holy Spirit will only confirm it. You are like God's vehicle on earth. He wants to drive you to his purpose. What is the point of purchasing a car and leaving it in the driveway? Usually when a car remains in the driveway over an extended period of time, this signifies that it may be broken—not working correctly. When we do not hear the voice of God, communion with God is broken—not working correctly. God desires to move

Chapter 6: Knowing the Secret Place

and do many excellent exploits through you. However, he will not move through you if he is unable to reveal his will to you. In Amos 3:7, the prophet says, "Surely the Lord GOD will do nothing, but he revealeth his secret unto his servants the prophets" (KJV). In this Scripture, the phrase that reads "servants the prophets" can also be translated *friends*.

God is doing many great things. Do you see the manifestation of these things in your life? If not, you may want to start hearing from God.

Now I believe your heart may be beginning to ask the more specific question: how can we hear God's voice? Hearing God's voice is like tuning your television to the weather station. If we want to know what to wear for the day, we tune in. Likewise, if we want to make spiritual preparation, we must channel our minds to the station of God. When you're in the secret place, the key to hearing God's voice is to listen.

In the secret place, you must hear beyond the fan blowing or kids playing outside. You must hear beyond your stomach growling and the silence. Then you will hear the voice of God.

Additionally, you must prepare to hear the voice of God. In the classroom, how does a teacher know you're listening? Can he tell by your posture or other actions? Someone whose focus is on his friends in the hallway is obviously not listening. But someone who is tediously writing down notes is.

While you are listening for the voice of God, have a pen and notepad with you. Have the Bible with you as well; God may desire to show you a passage in Scripture. Additionally, you may want to remove technological hindrances, particularly smartphones. Sometimes I will play a worship CD in the background. Finally, listen with great anticipation. God will speak and often will have more to say than your human mind can remember.

Listening to God is not complicated. Listening to God is simple. There are many books that provide excellent

Chapter 6: Knowing the Secret Place

insight on listening to the voice of God. I recommend *Let Us Pray* by Watchman Nee, *A Better Way to Pray* by Andrew Womack, *Rules of Engagement* by Cindy Trimm, *Power of the Tongue* by Bill Winston, and *The Prayer that Heals* by Francis MacNutt. But in the end, hearing from God ultimately boils down to you listening.

Someone has got to listen. The author of a book, your pastor, your spouse, or your mother will not be able to listen for you.

In these last days, it is particularly important to listen. I believe God's desire is for his children to be in a place where they don't have to turn on the television to find out the forecast. He will tell them in prayer. If they listen, he will warn them if danger is ahead; they will know on a certain day not to travel in that direction. Nor will they worry about shortages of food (Matthew 6:23). He wants his children to commune with him even in the simple, practical things of life.

"Communion with God" is only another way to say prayer or meditation. It's more than bread and wine, or crackers and grape juice. One of the purposes for communion is so God can reward you openly (Matthew 6:4). He is not only trying to make you spiritual. He also wants to put his power on display through your life. Even more, he sees you as an individual. There is a specific revelation, a specific direction, for your life. He has things for you that are beyond measure.

The Last Secret

When I was younger, one of my favorite pastimes was playing video games. The first few generations of games

Chapter 6: Knowing the Secret Place

were pretty simple. One of my favorite games was Pac-Man. My older sister and I would play that game for hours. The main point of the game was to clear all the pellets on the board and avoid the ghosts.

As video games progressed, they became more challenging. Most of the games you could still beat, but some games required manuals or what they called "walkthroughs" to beat. These walkthroughs would give you step-by-step directions on not only beating the game but also mastering it. These tips would reveal many hidden secrets within the game.

There were secrets within secrets.

Like a walkthrough, there is one more spiritual secret I would like to reveal to you. Actually, it's not a secret anymore, since Jesus revealed it many years ago to the Samaritan woman at the well in John 4. Toward the end of their conversation, she asked Jesus about worship. Her specific question was in regard to where should we worship. At the time, Jews believed that worship should take place in Jerusalem, while Samaritans worshiped in the mountain. She wanted to know the truth. Jesus responded by saying, "A time is coming and has now come when the true worshipers will worship the Father in the Spirit and in truth, for they are the kind of worshipers the Father seeks. God is spirit, and his worshipers must worship in the Spirit and in truth" (John 4:23–24 NIV).

So what is the last secret in this? What is the secret within the secret?

Our answer comes from poetry. In English class, we learned how to write poetry. There were many rules we needed to know to set our foundation. We learned what rhythm, meter, and feet were and their relationship to poetry. These elements gave tone, depth, and pace to our writing. Applying these rules helped us create poems.

As the semester progressed, our teacher then introduced the term *poetic license*. Poetic license is the liberty taken by a poet or other artist in deviating from a rule to produce a desired effect.

Chapter 6: Knowing the Secret Place

So occasionally we would deviate from the rule.

We would remove a rhyme or change how we stressed a syllable. It added creativity and allowed us to individualize our writings. This is the secret within the secret.

Instead of giving us poetic license, Jesus gives us a prayer license. In the beginning, we learn the foundation. We go into a room, we close the door, and we pray. But it doesn't have to be limited to that. This is not all that the tameion is. It's not simply a closed-off room. It doesn't have to be in a church building. The tameion can be in the midst of five thousand hungry women and children. It can be in a classroom as you prepare for a test. All that matters is that your prayer take place "in spirit and in truth."

Tradition will limit you. It will cause you to place God in a box. The Holy Spirit is so willing to move in you and through you! The apostle Paul knew God in this way. He encourages us in 1 Thessalonians 5:17 to "pray without ceasing." Don't let your physical location determine your spiritual destiny.

As you prepare to go to the secret place, I encourage you to take your time. Think of it as a process. Being raised in Western society, particularly here in the United States, we often expect immediate results. However, we should look at prayer and communing with God more like a marinating process. We must know it's working and practice patience as we wait for the manifestation. The longer we marinate in the presence of God through prayer, the better our relationship with him will be.

CHAPTER 7
KNOWING FAITH, HOPE, AND VISION

Chapter 7: Knowing Vision, Hope, and Faith

The sun had already set, and everyone in the house was asleep except me. The lights, the television, and even the radio were off. I was surrounded by total darkness with only the images from my imagination keeping me up. Tomorrow was the big day; my fifteen minutes of fame were just around the corner. Thoughts of what would transpire the next day marinated in my head as I rested on the bed. All the hours and effort I had put into perfecting my craft would pay off. There were many who had placed low expectations on me. They had even convinced my own flesh and blood that I was a pretender. However, if there was one thing I was confident in, this was it. My thoughts eventually came to an end as I slipped into sleep.

Before I knew it, the alarm sounded. The day seemed to pass in a flash. It was already 2:00 p.m. Everything before this moment seemed irrelevant. There I was, standing against the wall. The room was filled with sixteen warm bodies, sixteen anxious spirits. One stood out among them. We stood there as he encouraged us to execute in unity.

My mind began to focus on other thoughts. Words and images began to echo through my mind. *Worthless, good-for-nothing,* and *scrub*—which was the one I hated hearing the most—reverberated in my cerebellum. These words only fueled my determination. I could feel the blood in my neck boiling as I focused on the task at hand.

I heard people complaining about the smell. Perhaps they didn't have the same stakes I had. Maybe they had nothing to prove. But I did. This was near the end of the school year, and I had bragged all year that I was the best. My classmates were reminded daily of who I believed I was by looking at the button I had created for myself, labeled "Da Baller."

The button was the biggest they had ever seen. However, this button was not louder than my mouth. I bragged about my three-point shot, my defensive skills, and my long arms for rejecting my opponents' attempts at glory. Yes, I had nicknamed myself "Da Baller."

Chapter 7: Knowing Vision, Hope, and Faith

The more I talked, the better the stories became. No one could talk more stuff than I. On one occasion, I used my stories to alter the dictionary. It read "Da Baller," and the definition next to it was my name.

For years I had played basketball and even had a court in my backyard. Basketball was my daily bread. I watched it on television and played it on the video game system. And now I was prepared for glory. We exited the locker room and entered the high school field house.

It was my senior year, my last shot as we played the juniors. The game tipped off with me on the bench. The game went back and forth and was all tied at halftime. However, I had yet to see a second of action. The third quarter came and went, and I was still riding the pine. I began to think maybe our coach had let the perceptions of others influence his choice of rotation. He had to have heard it. Even some of my teammates didn't want me on the team. Not because of what I said but because of what others said. They believed I was a scrub. However, I knew something they didn't know. I also had something they didn't have, and that was hope. They had never played with me on the blacktops in the hood. They hadn't seen me hit those big three-point shots in the dark after the streetlights went out. I knew if given a chance, the truth would be revealed. I had faith.

Finally, with six minutes left in the game, Coach said, "Jamere, get in the game." Cheers and jeers came from the crowd as I left the bench. We were losing by ten points when I entered the game. The juniors in-bounded the ball and began to march it down the court. A grin came across my face as I looked at the guard, knowing what was about to take place. In a moment I stole the ball like a thief stealing a tourist's wallet on a crowded street in some country far away. In the twinkling of an eye, I laid the ball in the rim, just like I had envisioned it would happen. The crowd went wild; they couldn't believe their eyes. To make a long story short, we won the game.

Chapter 7: Knowing Vision, Hope, and Faith

A few months later, the yearbook came out. One of the editors gave me a book and told me to look on page fifty-eight. What I saw brought joy to my heart and still does even until this day. In the sports section, there is a picture of twenty of our school's best student athletes dressed in their athletic uniforms.

In the midst of those athletes stands yours truly in a regular T-shirt. The caption below the picture reads, "Who do you think the real Baller is?"

Me pictured to the right behind number 8

Who do you think the real baller is?

I wasn't good enough to earn a four-year scholarship, nor did I even possess the skills to play on the high school basketball team. But for one moment in time, I was the Baller.

There is a spiritual truth to be learned from this story of faith, hope, and vision. If I hadn't had these, I would not have accomplished my goal. *Faith, hope,* and *vision* are three distinct words that are closely connected. If you can understand their connection and execute it, your potential is limitless.

One of the best stories from Scripture that vividly illustrates this connection is the story of the woman with the issue of blood (Mark 5:25–34). This woman had a vision of being healthy and whole. She did everything possible to make this vision come to pass.

Chapter 7: Knowing Vision, Hope, and Faith

Vision: What You See Is What You Get

She looked at herself in the mirror. She was clothed in the finest white dress as she prepared to go to the festival. Everything was in its place: her hair, dress, makeup, and shoes. Her attention was drawn to the footsteps behind her. Her white dress, makeup, and hairstyle quickly faded to reality, like Cinderella when the clock struck midnight. Her focus left her image as she shifted to the words of the doctor.

"I'm sorry, there is nothing more we can do. We have tried nearly everything with the same results."

"But Doctor, there has got to be something else. Surely there is another remedy."

"We can try something else, but it will take more money."

"I'm broke. I have nothing left to give."

"Sorry, ma'am."

Something was missing in her life that she'd once had. She was missing wellness. All of her resources were consumed by her desire for wellness.

We can all relate to that feeling—*that* something is missing in our lives. Maybe we're missing some type of relationship, the perfect job, or good health. Maybe what's missing in our life is something we once possessed. Perhaps it's something we never had to begin with. When placed in this situation of need, we have a choice. We can search for what is missing or leave it void. What do you choose?

This woman chose to search for that missing thing. She had a vision. Vision is where your journey begins. The automobile, the airplane, and the cell phone were all formed from personal visions.

What is a vision? A vision is an image displayed in your mind. Visions come from three main sources: self, God, and the satanic realm. Your vision is the framework that will inspire you. Vision gives you direction (Habakkuk 2:2: "Then the LORD replied: 'Write down the revelation and make it plain on tablets so that a herald may run with it'" [NIV].). In the case of the woman with the issue of blood,

Chapter 7: Knowing Vision, Hope, and Faith

her vision was not written on paper but in her heart.

Many great people have accomplished great things as a result of their vision. Long ago there was a group of 260 men and five ships who had a vision of sailing around the world. Ferdinand Magellan was the visionary of the group. Only eighteen men survived to see the vision manifest. This vision broke them in every way possible, even killing Magellan. Following after your dreams and visions can break you. It can even kill you. Just ask Jesus. Hebrews 12:2 says that for the joy that was set before him (his vision of believers in the kingdom), he endured the cross. For Jesus, like Magellan, the vision was greater than the cost. And in the end, he gained everything by following it.

We all have visions and dreams. However, sometimes in life, our vision may become broken, distorted, or even snatched away. Maybe our vision is gone because someone told us we don't have the know-how or the resources to achieve or accomplish the task. Maybe we've given up on it because we feel insufficient, or maybe it is something impossible to the natural world.

How can we realize our vision? How can we make the impossible possible? Or perhaps a better question is, how can we make evident that which appears impossible to the natural eye? Hebrews 11:1 says, "Faith is the substance of things hoped for, the evidence of things not seen" (NIV).

Let's take our cue from CSI. Any detective knows that to prove your case, you need tangible evidence that can be measured in some fashion. Why? If there is no evidence, there is no proof that can connect the dots—or in our case, connect the eye to the impossible.

In the natural world, seeing is believing. The opposite is true in the spiritual world. In spirit, believing is seeing (2 Corinthians 4:13). One important truth that we must realize is that the spiritual world has more resources and substance than the natural world! The natural world was produced by the spiritual world (Job 38). This is why Paul prayed in Ephesians that the eyes of our hearts would be enlightened (Ephesians 1:18). He prayed this so that our

Chapter 7: Knowing Vision, Hope, and Faith

spiritual vision would come to realize the abundance of intangible resources accessible to us.

An example of this is recorded in the book of 2 Kings 6:17. A great army of horses and chariots surrounded Elisha and caused his servant, Gehazi, to fear greatly. But Elisha was confident because his vision enabled him to filter the spiritual into the natural. Seeing Gehazi's fear, he prayed that God would open the eyes of the young man. After the prayer, his servant's eyes became open, and he saw a mountain full of horses and chariots of fire all around them.

Just imagine Elisha's servant in that moment. How do you think this would have changed his perspective of his situation? How would it make him feel? Before his eyes were truly opened, he only saw doom, destruction, and darkness. But his perspective changed instantly. I would bet a new confidence arose within him. Suddenly he was no longer fearful for his life but confident and full of hope. This confidence was like that of the woman with the issue of blood who believed Jesus manifested the power to heal the sick.

More than a Dream: Visions of the Night

The artistic, cyan-colored sky and the trees stood in the background, as amazed as I was. I stood on the side of an empty highway, in the middle of nowhere. It was a beautiful day. I watched as a powerful force circled within itself, creating a strong gravitational pull. Its force howled past my ears. Normally one would run from such a thing. It is known for creating a path of destruction and chaos with each inch it takes. However, I was unafraid. As a matter of fact, seeing it brought a weird sense of comfort and control. I had never seen one in person, only on television. It was the mighty tornado.

Within moments, the tornado was gone. Suddenly a silver-back gorilla had me lying on the ground. I fought it with all my might as it viciously attacked my head. I swung harder and harder, kicking and scratching, attempting to

Chapter 7: Knowing Vision, Hope, and Faith

get it to release me. A voice from the background began to beckon my name. The voice grew clearer and clearer. She said, "Wake up, Jamere. You're dreaming and kicking me."

This was not the first time I'd had such a dream. On many occasions, I have awakened swinging, talking, and even singing. Fortunately for me, no one has been hurt by my swinging or singing! At one time in my life, I believed dreams were only the result of too many scary movies and/or junk food. It never occurred to me that they could be encoded messages sent from above . . . until I began to have them more frequently.

Dreams of bats, snakes, and spiders began to overtake me. Week after week, a familiar yet unfamiliar voice spoke to my dull ears and eyes. This voice yearned for me to take heed to its direction and revelation. In alien territory, I leaned on the familiar, the written Word of God. Surely Scripture has much to say about dreams. Additionally, my journalistic skills led me to scientists and philosophers who study dreams.

My findings were intriguing. Dreams have inspired beautiful ballads—like "Little Town of Bethlehem." They have also stretched their arm to science. Dmitri Mendeleyev gives credit to his discovery of the periodic table to a dream. But what does Scripture say about dreams? One of my favorite passages on the topic is Job 33:15–16:

> In a dream, a vision of the night,
> When sound sleep falls on men,
> While they slumber in their beds,
> Then He opens the ears of men,
> And seals their instruction. (NIV)

Our dreams are more than just entertainment for sleep. They provide direction through symbols. (This is not true of all dreams—some dreams may be the result of too much pizza. But many are much more than that.) These symbols are often confusing, and they may even seem nightmarish. King Nebuchadnezzar was troubled by a dream involv-

Chapter 7: Knowing Vision, Hope, and Faith

ing a statue (Daniel 2:1–3). Like myself, Nebuchadnezzar consulted those he perceived to be experts, the magicians. These experts were unable to unlock the meaning of his dream. As a matter of fact, they said it was impossible.

The king was so frustrated that he sent an execution order for all of the magicians. After hearing all that was going on, Daniel stepped into the picture and asked the king to give him time to interpret the dream. This dream was of a great image, a statue, and Daniel revealed that it represented Nebuchadnezzar's kingdom and kingdoms to come.

The Bible contains an assortment of dreams. The question today, however, is how can we extract wisdom from our dreams?

Investigating Dreams

As my dreams increased and became more troubling, I made several calls concerning them. I even had access to the meaning of symbols in dreams. One book said that bats represented demons or annoyances. Each animal and object had a meaning associated with it. I began to use these meanings as if they were pieces of a puzzle. Yet it just became more complicated. Finally, I spoke to a man who is considered an expert in dreams. He said the objects in our dreams are defined by our own personal experience. They are often based on our culture as well. In some cultures, bats represent something good. However, I found that some symbols from the dream are universal in meaning. For example, the white dove and water both represent the Holy Spirit. With nothing of substance to go on, I was back at square one. I was just like the king, troubled by these visions of the night. However, I didn't have a Daniel to guide me.

Over a time span of two years, my dreams and confusion only increased. I wondered if the prophecy of Joel 2 about dreams and visions was actually a good thing. These dreams seemed to serve no purpose but to torment me and produce a good conversation in the morning. I could

Chapter 7: Knowing Vision, Hope, and Faith

relate to Nebuchadnezzar being troubled! Then one day it hit me. I'm sure my sudden release was a result of the mercy of God through prayer and fasting. But what was once troubling was no longer troubling. What was once dark was now illuminated. What hit me, you may ask? Revelation. The meaning of my dreams was suddenly made known.

It was a few days after the dream of the tornado and the gorilla that attacked my head. I was in prayer before Wednesday-night Bible study, and I could feel the Holy Spirit pouring into me. I wrote down what he revealed. With each stroke of the pen, my heart was only comforted more. The mighty tornado represented the power of the Holy Spirit, while the gorilla symbolized the Enemy (the Devil) trying to destroy my mind. In both cases, I was on a highway . . . a road . . . a path. Each portion of the dream represented a path I could take. One path led to experiencing the power of the Holy Spirit moving mightily in my life. The other path led to death, where I would allow the Devil to take my wisdom from me.

The Holy Spirit said I would make this choice with my actions, by either walking in the Spirit or failing to do so.

The interpretation rang true. I felt like I had become Daniel overnight. But to what could I credit my success? Could it be from my journalistic investigations? Or was this newfound skill a result of what the dream expert had told me? Each, I believe, helped me figure out the meaning of the dream. But ultimately it was the Holy Spirit's doing. Yes, I know how you feel about that—whenever I hear someone say the Holy Spirit caused something, it seems like a cop-out. Please, can't you give me more information? The answer is vague. But there are things we can do to move the Holy Spirit on our behalf

One key to moving in this gifting is desire. I'm not talking about desire like the desire to go to a concert to hear your favorite band. It's a desire to go to a concert to see your favorite band when there are no tickets left and you are desperate to sit on the front row. It is what you need.

Chapter 7: Knowing Vision, Hope, and Faith

A *hungry* desire. Like when you're searching for your last few dimes to make a trip to the vending machine.

When you get this desire, the Holy Spirit will step in. Listen to what Daniel said to the king about interpreting dreams: Daniel said no wise man, enchanter, magician, or diviner could explain to the king the mystery of the dream (Daniel 2:27). There appeared to be no hope. But Daniel, who had the king yearning for every word, went on to say, "But there is a God in heaven who reveals mysteries" (Daniel 2:28 NIV). I love that verse! Daniel is speaking of the leading of the Holy Spirit. The wisdom to be gained from your visions of the night can be found in the Holy Spirit.

The Hope of a King

In some of the most powerful seventeen minutes in history, 200,000 to 300,000 people met for one purpose. They had the same vision, or in this case, dream. Each step they took was filled with purpose. With each breath, they inhaled destiny and exhaled the past. People of all backgrounds gathered at the nation's capital that day. They reverenced one individual as he painted the most beautiful picture without a canvas or paintbrush. His brush was his words, and his canvas the hearts of men. With each word he spoke, he drew an image of love and compassion. As he came toward the end of the speech, he began to focus more on his vision, his dream.

The crowd's hearts began to fill. Suddenly, his prepared speech began to take a turn. A famous gospel singer in the crowd named Mahalia Jackson shouted to the man giving his speech, "Tell them about the dream, Martin."

In that moment, Dr. Martin Luther King Jr. went from giving a prepared speech to preaching from his heart, punctuating each point by saying, "I have a dream." He dreamed that his children would not be judged by their outer appearance but by the content of their character. He dreamed that the sons of former slaves and slave owners would be able to sit and hang out together. As Dr. King

Chapter 7: Knowing Vision, Hope, and Faith

closed his speech, he told the crowd to go home not just with a dream, but also with hope. His exact words were, "This is our hope."

The great Dr. King, a student of Scripture, knew that vision produces hope. This hope is not the hope we have come to know. This hope is not the wishy-washy hope we reference when we say, "I hope it will rain" or "I hope my team wins." This is not the hope the dictionary refers to. Rather, it is a spiritual hope.

Our heavenly Father is always trying to produce hope in his children by giving us a vision. He told Abraham that his descendants would be as numerous as the stars in heaven or the sand on the seashore (Genesis 22:17). Just imagine a sky with no building to block your view! When Abraham looked up, do you think he tried to count? What about when he looked at the sand? Did he try to count its grains? We have all hoped in something. Hope is often viewed as less than faith. But what is hope? What distinguishes a biblical hope from a worldly hope? As a child, I was raised always to hope. I was taught that no matter how hard the wind blew against me, or how high the problem was, it would all work out. However, sometimes life can place us in a situation where there seems to be no hope.

It was the late '80s, and I was in middle school. I had just transferred to this school and moved to this neighborhood, so no one knew me. However, my father had just made me one of the coolest kids in school. I went to school looking like I had just left the Fort Knox jewelry store. The shine from my countenance should have made everyone I encountered wear sunglasses. My neck was heavy with two ice-gold (or as some would say, sterling silver) chains around my neck. One of them had a Mercedes Benz pendant with a diamond in the middle.

I received first-class treatment that day. First in line at the cafeteria, first one to be picked on the team, you name it, I was first. You know the saying: time flies when you're having fun. Well, that day it flew, and before I knew it, the school bell dismissed us. I didn't want the school day to

Chapter 7: Knowing Vision, Hope, and Faith

end. Nevertheless, I still knew I had a fifteen-minute walk home where I could flaunt my ice-gold chains.

As soon as I hit the door, a guy rushed me and snatched the chains off my neck. I stood there in shock as I watched him hand them over to a guy in a car as he drove off. Some of my classmates got the attention of the authorities, and I told them my story and ratted out the guy who had snatched my necklace. After a thirty-minute delay, I was free to go home. All of a sudden, the day that had been flying by was dragging. All the other students had already made their way home on the bus or by walking. So I would have to take the fifteen-minute walk home alone to ponder what had just happened.

Not even halfway through my walk, my day grew even darker. A kid walked up to me and said, "You may not want to go home that way," and he pointed in the direction I was headed. I looked down the hill, and about a block and a half down, I saw the car that had driven away with my necklace, the guy I had told on, and about four to five other older-looking guys. Quickly, the feeling that I wasn't going to make it home tried to overtake me. People killed people in the hood over matters like this. And to pile it on, this was the only way I knew to get home, since I was new to the area. This was before cell phones. I was in a hopeless situation. Then the kid quickly said, "Follow me. I will show you a way."

We walked in another direction about a half-block. Then we stopped. He pointed and said, "Cut through this house, go down about three blocks, make a right, and you will find your way." As he spoke, hope built up in me that I would live to see another day. I turned to thank the kid, but as quickly as he had appeared, he was gone, like he had vanished into thin air. I made it home that day and many more days after that. I know that God blessed me that day by sending one of his ministering angels for that assignment. In a place of no hope, there was hope.

Remember the vision that God was building in Abraham? It produced hope in Abraham.

Chapter 7: Knowing Vision, Hope, and Faith

Even later, in their old age, Abraham and his wife hoped in the promise God had made them of having their own child. Despite everything in the natural world pointing to the fact that it would be impossible for Sarah to have a son, guess what Abraham did? Romans 4:18 says, "Against all hope, Abraham in hope believed and so became the father of many nations, just as it had been said to him, 'So shall your offspring be.'" When there was nothing tangible to hope in, yet Abraham hoped. What distinguishes the hope of the world from a biblical hope is that a biblical hope does not disappoint (Romans 5:5). Additionally, we can have confidence in our hope based on the one who made the promise, our heavenly Father. One of my favorite Scriptures that points to this is Hebrews 6:13: "When God made his promise to Abraham, since there was no one greater for him to swear by, he swore by himself" (NIV). God will not leave you hanging when you place your confidence in him.

In the Old Testament, there is a story of hope and hopelessness that would affect an entire generation. Twelve spies were sent to the Promised Land to survey the land and give a report. After seeing the Promised Land flowing with milk and honey, but also spotting giants and fortified cities, ten of the spies brought back a vision of doom, gloom, and total destruction, causing the people to be fearful and have no hope (Numbers 14). However, the other two, Joshua and Caleb, brought back a vision of hope and even proclaimed that they would overcome the giants in the Promised Land (Numbers 13:30). But the people had already made their decision in their hearts, and the tribes were given what they chose, which was to wilt away in the desert (Numbers 14:28). True hope is a choice, a decision that is made within you.

The woman with the issue of blood had hope for wholeness. She said to herself, "If I can only touch the hem of his garment, I will be made whole" (Matthew 9:21, NIV). She had a biblical hope, not a wishy-washy hope. Biblical hope propels us into an action called faith.

Chapter 7: Knowing Vision, Hope, and Faith

H2O and Faith

Hope and faith may seem like interchangeable terms, but they are not. Hebrews 11:1 describes faith in two ways. First, faith "is the substance of things hoped for." This is one of the more famous passages in Scripture. But what does it mean?

Its meaning can be understood through the rarest chemical mixture in our solar system—which just happens to be abundant on earth. Water. When you look at a globe, you can see the juxtaposition between water and land. Scientists say water covers about 70 percent of the earth. This statement became relevant to me when I took my first cruise. As we inched away from land into the Atlantic Ocean, for miles and miles there was nothing but water. Water is vital for all forms of life on this planet. Without it, nothing could live. But how does water relate to hope and faith?

Hope can be compared to water, while faith is the molecules in the water. Without a microscope, we are unable to see the substance that forms water. Yet they hold water together. Faith works in the background, unifying hope.

Faith can also be compared to the director of a blockbuster movie. The director is the person who sets the tone of the movie and interprets the script as he sees it. He typically sees the story as a whole and gives it his own stamp. He instructs the actors on how to say their lines, make their facial expressions, and adjust their tone. Virtually anything that happens on a movie set is subject to the approval of the director. The final product is the direct result of decisions made by the director. That is what faith helps give you: a complete picture of hope, the final product.

Faith is also the "evidence of things not seen" (Hebrews 11:1). This brings to mind the story of the ten bridesmaids (Matthew 25). In this parable Jesus tells the story of a groom coming for ten bridesmaids. They were to prepare themselves by having oil in their lamps. All of the bridesmaids hoped the groom would come, but only

Chapter 7: Knowing Vision, Hope, and Faith

half were propelled into faith by filling their lamps with oil. Many have a form of hope, but how many of us have the hope that propels us into faith? This is one of the differences between faith and hope. Additionally, only half of the bridesmaids took action on their hope. They took action on what was not physically evident.

Building Your Faith

Someone once told me you build your faith by starting small, like asking God for a parking place in a crowded area. Many years ago, when I was about the age of twelve, something remarkable occurred. This event has served as a foundation of my faith for many years. It's not anything big, but for me it was.

My mother and my siblings were leaving the doctor's office. She decided to take an alternative route to search for a new home for us. As we walked down the block, an unchained pit bull came out of nowhere. Pit bulls are known to be very aggressive dogs, and the one we encountered fit the description. He ran toward us barking as he dragged his broken chain behind him. We were not about to outrun this dog, and I was less than three feet away from it. My mother immediately cried the name Jesus. Suddenly, the dog stopped barking. It sat down on the sidewalk as if someone had told it to sit. The dog seemed to be as confused and frozen as I was. "Go, Jamere, keep on walking," my mom said as she and my siblings hurried past the animal. My mother had faith that she could call on an unseen force to intervene in our daily lives. Her faith was in the name Jesus.

In the story of the centurion (Matthew 8:5–10), we see vision, hope, and faith at work. The centurion must have envisioned his servant well, and this vision produced a hope in him that propelled him to faith. He had the faith to ask Jesus for his servant's healing. We all hope, but how many of us let that hope propel us into faith? How many of us are like the woman with the issue of blood who envisioned herself being healed by touching the hem of

Chapter 7: Knowing Vision, Hope, and Faith

his garment? Her vision produced a hope that propelled her into faith to press through the multitudes. Her vision changed not only her body but also how we perceive her. We know her not as the woman who was sick but the woman who was healed.

What Does Jesus Look For?

Having faith, hope, and vision will not only affect your vision of yourself, but it will also affect those around you as well. Faith is not easy to walk out; it is often like going against the grain. Faith is rare in these days—true faith, that is.

Jesus is always seeking those who possess faith. That's why he asked who touched him when the woman reached out for his garment. And remember what he told the people about the centurion's faith? "When Jesus heard this, he was amazed at him, and turning to the crowd following him, he said, 'I tell you, I have not found such great faith even in Israel'" (Luke 7:9 NIV). He was looking for it. Jesus searches for faith like a slave searches for freedom.

There are many things recorded in Scripture solely for our generation. Daniel wrote prophecies meant for us, not for him (Daniel 12:4). He was only the messenger. Jesus posed a question toward the disciples. This question was only for them to record; it was meant for us. In Luke 18:8, he asks, "When the Son of Man returns, will he find faith?"

We have been presented with a choice. Will you be like the wise bridesmaids whose vision and hope propelled them into faith? Or will you be like the other five?

Vision, hope, and faith work hand in hand. They work with one accord to manifest the spiritual world into the present, natural, time-bound world. Or as Romans 4:17 says, "As it is written: 'I have made you [Abraham] a father of many nations.' He is our father in the sight of God, in whom he believed—the God who gives life to the dead and calls into being things that were not" (NIV).

CHAPTER 8
KNOWING TO WAIT

Chapter 8: Knowing to Wait

They said the church service would last no longer than two hours. We were all given a program, or as I refer to it, a to-do list. It was my guide to freedom. As the program progressed, I placed a check mark beside each element. Invocation ... check. Scripture reading ... check. Church history ... check. Choir number one ... check. Praise dance number one ... check.

As the service went on, my hopes of a timely escape fell. Each choir was only to sing one song, but the first choir said a spirit inspired them to sing two more. However, that wasn't the longest part. What made the service even longer was the need the MC and everyone else whose sole purpose was to give an introduction felt to preach for five minutes. My eyes scanned the crowd, back and forth, looking to see who was still awake. The ceiling and hand fans had no effect. It was a Sierra Desert heat in there. The children uninvolved in the service were playing games. Babies cried, and deacons were having their own side conversations.

Finally, it was the minister's time to speak. He must have just purchased one of those motivational quote books, because it seemed like he was trying to string in as many quotes as possible. The people in the pews grew restless as he told story after story. A few people even told him to shut up—literally. Two hours had already passed. I could no longer take it. I walked out of the service and headed home.

Later that evening, my friend called me. He said I had missed one of the most powerful altar calls ever, all because I had refused to wait.

Waiting is one of the more frequent and difficult tasks in life. We are always in some state of waiting. Waiting to be paid, waiting for the bus, waiting to eat, you name it. The question I have is: What are you doing while waiting? Are you complaining? Are you waiting impatiently? Since life is full of waiting, it is important to discover what Scripture says about it.

We will begin by exploring the origins of waiting.

Chapter 8: Knowing to Wait

Waiting has been around since the beginning of creation. Adam waited for the plants of the garden to grow and mature. He waited for the animals to stand before him as he named them.

He even waited for God to form him a mate.

The Waiting Game

Waiting has been here from the start. However, waiting was never a problem in paradise. Maybe everyone had a good dose of patience. Things changed quickly after the fruit was eaten. God pronounced judgment and cursed the earth. The world was now in a fallen state. God kicked the people out of the garden. Eventually, man's body would return to dust.

Something else changed that is often overlooked. That is the process of waiting. Waiting became a challenge and a long process instead of the beautiful process it had once been. Time no longer worked in harmony with man; instead, it served as a reminder of our limited days. Time, in a sense, became an enemy of man. The dictionary defines *time* as a limited period or interval. In the distant past, time was measured by the rotation of the earth. Later, in the 1600s, man began to use the pendulum to measure time to the very minute. Today in Colorado, they use atoms to measure time. As the atom vibrates or ticks, it gives off vibrations of light. Each one of those vibrations represents a nanosecond. Yet, for all our sophisticated ways of measuring it, time is still a mystery. We can't see or touch time, but we feel it slip by. Clocks can tell us what time has passed, but they cannot tell us what time is. Even the greatest scientists of our day still debate this question. The great Albert Einstein concluded that the past, present, and future all exist simultaneously. Whatever the case, when we think of the bigger picture, we can see that time is simply a tool in the hands of God.

God is eternal, and he uses time as a funnel to execute what is already done in heaven: "Since all of the promises of the Lord are yes and amen" (2 Corinthians 1:20 NIV).

Chapter 8: Knowing to Wait

He has already done all that needs to be done. However, he waits for certain things to develop within time. This is what theologians refer to as a *dispensation*. God operates in dispensations. He arranges events, people, and other spiritual elements through the funnel of time. Of course he could do it all at once, but mankind as a whole is not ready to receive full revelation.

How God operates can be compared to a photographer. Long ago (maybe just over fifteen years ago), photographers used what they called darkrooms. When I was a photography student, we would take a picture on an SLR film camera. Then we took the roll into a literally dark room. Once in the darkroom, we were able to remove the film from the camera, since light could expose the images and render them useless. The film would go through a series of steps involving several types of chemicals, a photo enlarger, and wet, drying, and fixing stages. After all of that, you would have your perfect image. The image would be unable to process all of the chemical solutions at once. Trying to make it do so would badly alter the image. Developing a picture was a process, a waiting game. But in the end you would have your desired result.

The Bible has a spectrum of stories of people who have waited for different things for different reasons. In preparation for the Last Supper, Jesus told his disciples there would be a man carrying a jar of water waiting for them (Mark 14:12–26). Elijah stood on the mountain waiting for the Lord to pass by (1 Kings 19:11). Waiting involves what I call the three Ws: waiting, waiting, and more waiting. Even in manifesting our destiny, there is a season of waiting. If we look at waiting as a hindrance, we have missed its purpose.

Types of Waiting
One of the most common Scriptures on waiting can be found in Isaiah 40:31: "But they that wait upon the LORD shall renew their strength; they shall mount up with wings as eagles; they shall run, and not be weary; and they shall

Chapter 8: Knowing to Wait

walk, and not faint" (NIV). The Hebrew word for "wait" here is *qavah*. This word has two layers of revelation. The first revelation is that to wait is to look for, hope, expect. Is this how we wait? Do we expect? Do we hope? Or do we have a critical wait? You know, the kind when you look at the time, saying, "I'm only going to give them one more minute." This is exactly what happened to Saul in 1 Samuel 13. Saul had just been crowned as king, and soon he would be tested.

One of Saul's sons acted foolishly by attacking a Philistine outpost. Expecting trouble, Saul assembled an army at Gilgal. Likewise, the Philistines gathered their army and came against the Israelites to fight. Saul had been directed by the prophet Samuel to do nothing until he arrived. Samuel, the prophet of God, was to come and bless the battle by offering a burnt sacrifice. Saul waited for the time set by Samuel. But we can tell that Saul did not wait with hope but with despair. His men, sensing King Saul's despair, began to flee in fear. They lost courage and hid in caves and surrounding towns. The seventh day arrived, and Samuel was nowhere in sight. Tired of waiting, Saul took matters into his own hands and offered a burnt sacrifice to God. Saul knew that unless a sacrifice was offered, they would face certain defeat. Just when Saul had finished the offering, guess what happened? You guessed it! Samuel came. The rest of the story goes like this:

> Just as he finished making the offering, Samuel arrived, and Saul went out to greet him. "What have you done?" asked Samuel. Saul replied, "When I saw that the men were scattering, and that you did not come at the set time, and that the Philistines were assembling at Mikmash, I thought, 'Now the Philistines will come down against me at Gilgal, and I have not sought the Lord's favor.' So I felt compelled to offer the burnt offering." "You have done a foolish thing," Samuel said. "You have not kept the command the Lord your God gave you; if you had, he would have established your kingdom over Israel for all time. But

Chapter 8: Knowing to Wait

now your kingdom will not endure; the Lord has sought out a man after his own heart and appointed him ruler of his people, because you have not kept the Lord's command." (1 Samuel 13:10–14 NIV)

There is a destiny and purpose for all of us that is moments around the corner. But if we don't learn what God means when he says, "Wait upon the Lord," then we, like Saul, will lose our appointment with destiny. We must learn how to wait. Abraham also had to learn how to wait. Neither his nor Sarah's actions were perfect as they waited on the promised son. But they eventually got their act together, and they received the promise.

Another worthy story worth considering is the wait of Noah.

In Genesis 6:5, we read, "The Lord saw how wicked the Earth had become." If you think it's corrupt in Watts, Vatican City, or Wall Street, they have nothing on Noah's hood! Just imagine how Noah felt. This was a very wicked time, so wicked that God saw it as necessary to destroy the earth completely! When we read about Noah, it should inspire us and give us confidence that we too can survive and strive. He was the last righteous man in a world that had become corrupt.

Noah must have witnessed the world grow even more corrupt throughout his lifetime. Surely in the midst of his daily activities, he was waiting for a response from God. Perhaps he was waiting for a word or for God to destroy all the wicked people. We often focus on the time Noah spent waiting for it to rain after God had told him he would flood the earth. But what about the time it took for God to respond to what was occurring on the earth, before God gave him instructions to build the ark?

What do you think Noah was doing during that time? Was he complaining? Maybe he hid for his life. Maybe he prayed for God to take him away like his grandfather Enoch. Either way, he must have been waiting for God to do something. Scripture does not allude to what was

Chapter 8: Knowing to Wait

transpiring in the mind of Noah.

In times of waiting, I have often resorted to the easiest option, which is complaining. I'm not an in-your-face person, but I am good at inward complaining. This is the complaining we do in our minds.

Though we're not voicing it, it still has the same effect. When I watching the evening news and observe all the injustice throughout the world, the kidnapping, murders, rapes, orphans, and wars, I'm wondering, *How long is God going to let this happen*? My thoughts are much like those of the prophet Habakkuk in his own day:

How long, Lord, must I call for help, but you do not listen? Or cry out to you, "Violence!" but you do not save? Why do you make me look at injustice? Why do you tolerate wrongdoing? Destruction and violence are before me; there is strife, and conflict abounds. Therefore the law is paralyzed, and justice never prevails. The wicked hem in the righteous, so that justice is perverted. (Habakkuk 1:1–4 NIV)

Scripture doesn't allude to it, but I don't believe Noah complained. As a matter of fact, the Bible says that Noah was perfect and even found favor with God. What was he doing to earn such a reputation? Why did God call him perfect? This is where we come to our second revelation of waiting. The word *qavah* not only means a wait of expecting, but it also means "to bind together." Qavah is also used in Jeremiah 3:17: "At that time Jerusalem shall be called the throne of the Lord, and all nations shall *gather/qavah* together, to the presence of the Lord in Jerusalem, they shall no more stubbornly follow their own evil hearts" (NIV). This gathering is not like the people who gather around Times Square. This gathering is referring to people gathering in one accord, coming together with a single purpose. Let's look at the Scripture Isaiah 40:31 again with a different revelation: "Those who bind together with the Lord shall renew their strength." But what does that

Chapter 8: Knowing to Wait

mean? It means that you are not just waiting on God, but you are waiting *with* God. When you wait on God, you are becoming one with God. It's as if God is weaving or engrafting himself into you. This is what was going on with Noah. As Noah waited, God engrafted himself into him, causing Noah to become perfect. The time of waiting created a perfect union between him and God.

We often meet our best friends when we are waiting. I was on the campus of Lincoln University, waiting for a session to begin. There were a few other people there, but I began to talk to a gentleman named Brian. As we waited for the meeting to begin, we began to learn of each other's backgrounds and campus experiences and how we had arrived at our location. During this time of waiting, we formed a brotherhood, though at the time we didn't realize it. Times of waiting deepened our ties over the years. On some occasions we spent hours driving as we waited to arrive at our destination for a mission. We went on several mission trips to Texas and Atlanta. We have become brothers. My son calls him uncle, and I call his children my nieces and nephews. We are there for each other.

Understanding waiting in this way brings another dimension to many stories in Scripture. One of those is the story of Daniel. The prophet Daniel sent a request to the Lord. Daniel had a vision of a great war and wanted to know the meaning of his dream. Scripture says that for three weeks, Daniel waited on a response from God. During those twenty-one days, God was unifying himself with Daniel. Daniel yielded to God by abstaining from choice foods, wine, and lotion. His yielding allowed God to intertwine with him. (You can read the whole story in Daniel 10). Second Chronicles 7:14 also reflects this view of waiting: "If my people, who are called by my name, will humble themselves and pray and seek my face and turn from their wicked ways, then I will hear from heaven, and I will forgive their sin and will heal their land." In other words, God is saying, "If my people would strive

Chapter 8: Knowing to Wait

to become one with me, the following would happen." Instead of God waiting on his people, God will be waiting with his people. God will become one with them. When God is one with his people, not only are his people healed, but the land is healed.

I have come to the realization that God is not waiting until our knees are dirty and in pain from bowing in prayer. He is not waiting to see how loud our stomachs are growling because we are fasting. He is always ready to answer prayers. God's desire to manifest himself to you is greater than your desire to see him. Yet, in the same breath, why do we deserve to see or hear God if we can't wait for him?

Learning to Wait

In my current position at the university where I work, I'm a training coordinator. I tell the students on campus that not only am I your teacher, but I'm your teacher's teacher. I teach a few adjunct courses in technology. But my primary responsibility is to teach faculty how to implement technology in their courses. These faculty members are experts in their field, whether it be history, nursing, natural science, etc. But when it comes to implementing technology, I am the master. I have encountered many teachers who were never taught the proper way to use certain technology. I had this same issue when it came to waiting on God: I didn't really know how to do it. I had to learn to properly implement waiting on God. For many years, I was not taught how to wait on God.

I just always expected that after I did my part, his response would eventually come.

However, waiting on God should be done in a certain way. Remember our first revelation about waiting? There should be a conscious expectation that God will respond. Habakkuk 2:2 says, "For the revelation awaits an appointed time; it speaks of the end and will not prove false. Though it linger, wait for it; it will certainly come and will not delay" (NIV).

Chapter 8: Knowing to Wait

It will certainly come. This is how the centurion responded to Jesus (Matthew 8:5–13). The centurion came seeking a healing for his servant. He told Jesus, "I'm unworthy to have you come to my house, but just send your word." Jesus responded to this by saying, "I have not found so much faith" (Matthew 8:10 NIV). The centurion practiced waiting as he returned home to where his servant was. During this walk back, he was waiting in certainty.

Something else that stood out to me as I studied this concept was the second part of Habakkuk 2:2: "Though it linger, wait for it; it will certainly come and will not delay." How are we to understand the idea of something lingering but not delaying? The answer is in the story of the flood. God responds to the corruption of the world by telling Noah, "I am going to put an end to all people, for the earth is filled with violence because of them. I am surely going to destroy both them and the earth" (Genesis 6:13 NIV). The thing that was not delaying was the judgment: you could bank on it. But what about the lingering? In this case, the lingering was 120 years. Many scholars believe that it was 120 years from the time God told Noah to build the ark until the day it began to rain (Genesis 6:13–14). During those 120 years while Noah and his sons built the ark, he faced many obstacles. Surely the people discouraged him as they watched and mocked him. Did Noah need 120 years to build the ark? No one knows. Maybe yes, maybe no. They were a time of lingering. The Father was giving people a chance to repent. In this case, the time of lingering was a time of grace.

Another case of delay and lingering was when Daniel waited those three weeks. Daniel prayed, and God answered his prayer as soon as it left his lips—the answer did not delay. Yet there was a three-week lingering. The Enemy interfered with God's response, resulting in the need for Daniel to linger.

Satan is involved in hindering prayers and prolonging the waiting process. When the angel finally arrived,

Chapter 8: Knowing to Wait

Daniel was told that for three weeks a spiritual battle had raged on (Daniel 10:13). In the cases of Daniel and Noah during their time of waiting, they were becoming one with the Father.

Another person who had an expectant wait for a promise was Simeon. Described as righteous and devout, Simeon waited on God for the coming of the Messiah (Luke 2:25–38). He was an older man. What I love most about this story is that Simeon had been given a promise. The Holy Spirit promised Simeon that he would not die until he saw the "consolation of Israel," the coming Messiah. God spoke to Simeon sometime between the Old and New Testaments. Theologians have labeled this time period as the silent years, when there was no revelation from God. However, those who have an open heart to God will see and hear even when others experience only silence. I wonder how long he waited for this promise. Was he a teenager or a middle-aged adult when he heard? Apparently he waited for a long time. In the end, his expectation was fulfilled.

In the Meantime

All of these heroes of the faith were waiting on a promise. These promises would take them to an expected destiny. However, there is a challenge in waiting on the promise. I once heard someone say the following prayer: "O Lord, I know you will help us; but will you please help us before you will help us?" The challenge is the meantime.

What is the meantime? It's the distance between point A and point B. When you are in a period of waiting for the promise, you feel powerless. Being in a state of waiting places you in an environment where you feel like a child, dependent on someone else. There were many times in my childhood when I waited on something promised, and it never happened. Once my aunt told me she would bring my cousins over the next day to play with me. With great anticipation I woke up the next morning, took a bath, and waited as I watched Saturday morning cartoons. Lunch

Chapter 8: Knowing to Wait

came, and I knew the time was near for them to come. I went outside to sit on the porch. Listening to the sounds of the cars driving by raised my expectations. But when I saw that it wasn't their car, my countenance changed.

The day began to pass, with the sun going down as I sat at the top of the steps. Finally, my mother came outside and said she didn't think they were coming. They never came. It was a promise unfulfilled.

We all have been in this meantime state, when we are waiting for the promise. Your promise may have come from a loved one. It may have been from a prophet or from the Word of God. This promise may be for a car, a healing, or the salvation of a loved one. Regardless, it's a promise. When a good amount of time has passed and the promise has not happened, it can lead to discouragement. Proverbs 13:12 says, "Hope deferred makes the heart sick" (NIV). Such heartsickness can make you weary or even cause you to become sarcastic about the promise. Regrettably, all of us lack faith in some areas of our lives. Sarah began to laugh at God sarcastically when she heard the promise that she would have a son.

Some say Sarah lost her faith. Instead, we should look at this from a different angle. Her faith was hidden, buried by time and fear. Fearing the promise will not happen often causes us to bury what God has given us. We bury the promise by saying, "God can do it, but will he?" We believe that if we repress the promise, it will no longer hurt us. In the parable of the talents, this is what happened to one of the servants (Matthew 25:24). The master gave talents (large quantities of money) to three of his servants, and when he returned, each of them had produced a result except one. It says in Matthew 25:24–25, "Then the one who had received the one talent came forward and said, 'Master, I knew you were a demanding person, harvesting where you did not plant and gathering where you did not scatter; so out of fear I went off and buried your talent in the ground. Here it is back'" (NIV).

Chapter 8: Knowing to Wait

Instead of investing his talent, he buried it. He accused the master of being harsh. He even suggested that God is lazy and takes credit where no credit is due. He said to God, "You didn't plant it, but you take it." He accused God. But in reality, the servant was the lazy one. The other servants were willing to invest the time and effort in growing their talents, while he was not. We must not bury the promise our heavenly Father has given us as we wait. Don't let the worries and issues of life bury the Word. Don't let them choke what the Master Gardner has placed into you. In times of waiting, I encourage you to grow closer to God through prayer, fasting, worship, and the study of the written Word. During this time, focus on the promise. Something I do is print off a picture I have found on the Internet of what I'm waiting for, or I will write a story about how I feel after receiving the promise. These small things help me hold on while I'm waiting on the promise.

Manifesting the Sons of God

Twelve years of hard work had finally ended. It was a beautiful graduation ceremony. Walking across the stage had never brought such joy as the principal handed me my diploma. It was a happy time to celebrate with my friends and family. Some of my closest high school friends decided to combine funds and rent a limo for the night. After the graduation, we said our last good-byes to teachers and classmates we would never see again. We sat in the lobby conversing as we awaited our limo, which was already thirty minutes late.

My sister asked me if I was sure I didn't need a ride. But we were confident the limo would arrive shortly. Finally, we decided to call the rental company, and to our pleasant surprise, the limo was waiting on us. The driver had parked to the side of the convention center due to traffic. There were several other graduations going on at the time. People, cars, and limos cluttered the area. But our transportation was already there. We were waiting on someone who was waiting on us. Usually when we think

Chapter 8: Knowing to Wait

of waiting, we think of us waiting on God to move. But Scripture shows that nine times out of ten, it's God waiting on us. Isaiah 30:18 says, "And therefore will the LORD wait, that he may be gracious unto you, and therefore will He be exalted, that he may have mercy upon you: for the LORD is a God of judgment: blessed are all they that wait for him" (NIV).

Yes, the Creator of all that is known is waiting on us! Jesus stands at the door and knocks, and not just in relation to our salvation. He is waiting for us to answer the calling on our lives. He is waiting for the church to humble themselves; he is waiting for his people to turn from their wicked ways (2 Chronicles 7:14). Then he will do what he has always desired to do. He will bring healing to the people and to the land. When I was younger, one of my favorite shows was *The Incredible Hulk*. Matter of fact, I thought the Hulk was a real person. My uncle, father, and mother would attempt to sway me from what I believed as fact. There was no way they could convince me because I had seen it firsthand on television.

The Incredible Hulk was centered on a scientist named David Banner. He was no ordinary scientist. There was a power lying dormant within him. This power could only be activated through anger. Like the Hulk, there is a power in us that God and creation are waiting for us manifest. But what unlocks the power within you? For each of us, it is something different. This is a road you must take on your own through prayer and fasting. One key I will give you is desire (1 Corinthians 12:31 NIV). The Creator of all that is known and unknown waits for the created. In the parable of the ten virgins, it says the bridegroom was delayed. Why? Was there a spiritual traffic jam in heaven that caused this delay? Maybe his chariot got a flat? No, his delay was intentional. The groom knew of the five who were not prepared and wanted to give them time. Eventually the groom could no longer delay, though; he had a promise to keep to the other five.

Chapter 8: Knowing to Wait

The time is near when the Groom will no longer delay. The Groom today is soon to return, and he will return to a bride without spot or wrinkle (Ephesians 5:27). Will you be prepared?

CHAPTER 9:
KNOWING EMPTINESS

Chapter 9: Knowing Emptiness

It was a nice, warm summer day, a good day to hang out with friends. With my friends Dre, JD, and JD's girlfriend, Lisa, I went to the mall to go shopping. Lisa didn't really hang out with us normally, but I thought her presence would make for an interesting day. Right away I realized this was a bad idea. As we stood in the greeting card store looking for a card, I spotted a sinister smile on Lisa's face. She had placed several cards and a few other items in her purse. I could see where this was headed, and I didn't want to end up there, so I separated myself from the group by going to the food court.

About twenty minutes later, an officer came to me and said, "We have evidence of you stealing." He took me to the security office located on the ground floor. Things appeared to have taken a very wrong turn. As I entered the room, Dre was sitting to my right, and JD and Lisa were toward the back speaking with another officer. Dre and I made disconsolate attempts to free ourselves, but our words had no effect on the officer. The evidence was against us. There was a video of us all walking together in several stores. It appeared to be a done deal. We were guilty by association.

The officer then approached JD and asked, "What about these two?" JD said, "Let them go. They have nothing to do with it." The officers asked him if he was sure. "Let them go!" JD said.

We attempted to explain what had really happened, but the officer said, "Leave the premises now before you go down too." A few days later, I discovered that JD had taken the rap for Lisa. He would soon be doing time. He made a sacrifice for her, and not just for her but also for his friends. Dre and I could have faced the same criminal charges simply by our association. JD accepted a burden so his friends might be released.

This type of sacrifice is uncommon in today's world. Long ago, there lived a man who made a much greater sacrifice. This person possessed no guilt, nor had he committed any crime. He was wrongfully condemned, and his

Chapter 9: Knowing Emptiness

own friends allowed it to go down (Zechariah 13:6). Even though he knew this would happen, it still had to hurt him. Imagine being in the courtroom, and your friends know of your innocence. Yet they play a vital role leading toward your condemnation. Any other man would no doubt have desired revenge. But his words on the cross were, "Forgive them, for they know not what they do" (Luke 23:24 NIV). How could he do this? What within him could cause him to be this strong? The surprising answer is that there was nothing in him. Scripture says Jesus emptied himself (Philippians 2:7).

This is a very special statement because Scripture also says that God desires us to empty ourselves. Perhaps another word is to sacrifice (Romans 12:1). But what does sacrifice look like for a believer? It comes in many variations, and it's an important part of manifesting our destiny.

Emptying Yourself

One type of sacrificing is fasting. There are many methods of fasting. Once, while listening to the radio, I heard of a media fast. This fast involves abstaining from playing video games, watching television, and other forms of media entertainment. Others choose a more select fast. Some individuals may go on a caffeine fast. Others may go on an all-salad fast because they really love meat. It really depends on the person. I know individuals who have no problem going without food and will go on an Internet fast instead. Daniel and the three Hebrew boys chose a select fast where they only ate certain foods (Daniel 1).

Fasting is more than just abstaining from something you desire. When you perceive fasting only as not eating, you're not fasting, you're just starving. Additionally, fasting is not a tool that causes God to move; rather, it's a tool that changes you. Before Jesus began his earthly ministry, he fasted for forty days and forty nights. What was his purpose? Jesus understood that fasting is a key to the supernatural. During Jesus' fast, he encountered both

Chapter 9: Knowing Emptiness

demons and angels. I heard one evangelist on the radio say that you are bound to become delusional when you abstain from food. But fasting is more than that, and the experiences that can happen while you fast are more than delusions.

Anyone who believes that does not understand the purpose of fasting. I like to compare fasting to shoveling snow. My flesh prefers to do neither. However, if I want to go anywhere spiritually or physically, both are required. I have a long driveway, and when it snows, there is much to shovel. One day last year it snowed four inches, which is not a lot compared to the sixteen inches a couple of years ago! But those four inches of snow were enough to keep me from leaving my driveway. Usually when it snows, I scatter ice melt down the path. This does not rid me of the snow, but it softens it, making it easier to remove when shoveling.

Fasting is like throwing that salt. Fasting softens the cares of the world that block out spiritual awareness. However, fasting in itself is not the answer. You must also have communion with the Father while fasting. When you have communion with God, you allow God to shovel the cares away.

Fasting causes many wonderful things to transpire. When Daniel fasted and prayed for twenty-one days, something marvelous happened on both the first and twenty-first days. On the first day, the prayer was answered. On the twenty-first, the message was delivered. Daniel had no idea what was transpiring for twenty days, but at the time, a great angelic conflict was occurring in the spiritual world. On the twenty-first day, Daniel was still strong enough to sit up, but he was quickly brought to his knees. Fear brought an uncontrollable shaking upon him as he attempted to regain his posture and stand up in the presence of an angel. This angel brought to Daniel the interpretation of a dream that frightened him. After Jesus fasted, he was met with angels who provided food (Matthew 4:11). At the end of Moses' fast, he received the

Chapter 9: Knowing Emptiness

Ten Commandments (Exodus 34:28).

During a time of fasting, God's desire is to place something within you. For each of us, God will manifest differently. When I fast, I have dreams. These dreams are so vivid I can still recall the emotions I felt, the words that were spoken, and sometimes even smells I encountered after I wake up.

Recently I went on a three-day fast from food. I still drank water and tea. During lunch, I read Scripture and wrote notes. At night, however, God would speak to me through my dreams (Job 33:15). On the second night of my fast, I found myself in a police car in the position of an officer. Another officer was driving as I sat in the passenger's seat. We rode around the city as if this was our normal routine. Then we received an APB, which is police talk for "be on the lookout for this guy." He was said to be in our vicinity, armed and dangerous.

As soon as we received his whereabouts, we went in pursuit. The officer driving the car was flying. I could feel the high wind coming into the window because of our speed. I held on to the bottom of the seat. It felt like we were going warp speed. In moments, the suspect was in view, and he was indeed armed and dangerous. However, as we came closer, I was able to see a complete picture of the suspect. He was armed and dangerous, but he looked like he suffered from malnutrition. He struggled to hold his weapons and take aim.

Immediately, I awoke. Usually I have to pray and wait awhile for the interpretation of a dream. But the Holy Spirit quickly made clear to my spirit what I had just seen.

The car going into warp speed symbolized God moving me deeper and faster into spiritual discernment. However, I was told that only living a life of continual fasting and praying would fulfill this.

Beyond this, I saw that the enemy was a representation of my enemy. He is armed and dangerous, but if you can really see him, you'll realize he has no power (Colossians 2:15).

Chapter 9: Knowing Emptiness

Going without food is not the only type of sacrifice available to us. Sacrifice comes in many shapes, sizes, colors, and hairstyles. When I think of sacrifice, my grandmother quickly comes to mind. For many years, I had no idea this person with whom I lived had sacrificed so much. I knew she had traveled a long way to get here. She was from the other side of the globe. There were many customs and traditions she had set aside to come to the United States of America. Of course she had changed her diet. She no longer had many of the traditional cuisines she had grown accustomed to. They were now distant memories.

What about all of her relatives? As far as she was concerned, her mother, father, siblings, and cousins were no closer to her than a rock on the planet Mars. She no doubt felt like an alien, unable to speak to anyone in Tagalog, one of her native tongues. Authorities even discouraged her from teaching her children this language. Little by little, her identity was sponged away. Even her long, beautiful hair was cut to less than half its length.

However, this was a sacrifice she took so her children and the generations who came after her could benefit.

Adel Spencer
(my grandmom)
& Vincil Spencer
(my aunt)

To her, leaving her home was a sacrifice worth making. She understood how giving works, and my grandmother was a very spiritual woman.

Chapter 9: Knowing Emptiness

My father once told me he had seen her giving money to a homeless guy. He asked her, "Why are you giving money to this stranger?" Her reply was, "Because someday you will need it."

Emptying Our Cup

My grandmother understood the path to emptiness and the destiny that lies beyond it. She understood that sacrifice in itself is not the end. Many monks practice the path of emptiness. They empty themselves of the world and everything connected with it so that when they are empty, then God can fill them. However, many monks are missing something. They have nowhere to release what God has placed within them because they have isolated themselves from those who need filling.

There was once a monk who emptied himself so much that you could see the filling of God's mighty power within his life. He is known as St. Benedict of Nursia. St. Benedict grew up in a wealthy family in Rome. He was very privileged, lacking nothing; he even had servants. However, there was something missing in his life. He was a believer, but he desired more of God. This led him to live a life of seclusion for three years. During this time, God filled him. However, he did not stay in seclusion! He is known for performing many great miracles. He raised people from the dead, cast out demons, and healed a boy of leprosy. Once, he prophesied to a king named Totila that he would die in ten years because of his wickedness, which was fulfilled. St. Benedict was so influential that he was seen as a threat to the church. They tried to assassinate him several times. Once they tried to poison him with a drink, but as he prayed over the drink, the cup shattered. Another time they poisoned his bread; however, a raven came and took it from his plate. St. Benedict was able to perform many of these miracles because he had emptied himself, which allowed God to fill him. He was so filled that he could manifest the power within him and transfer it to someone else.

Chapter 9: Knowing Emptiness

This is the purpose of becoming empty: it is so you can become filled. We must continually empty ourselves so God can continually fill us. Those of us who want to see the sick healed, the dead raised, and the people come into communion with God must empty ourselves. This is the same understanding Jesus possessed. He knew the cross in itself was not the end. He knew the grave would not hold him. But more important to him was the redemption of his brothers and sisters. His sacrifice gave him joy because he knew someday we would reign together with him (Hebrews 12:2).

Often true sacrifice involves us giving up what we desire most. For one it might be a donut, for another it might be a thousand dollars, and for another it might be one hour of your time a day. For others it is so much more. Here in the United States, we are blessed to have freedom of religion (for the time being). We are blessed to publicly worship the God who loves us so much. But it is not like that everywhere. In some countries, people sneak to hidden places to read the Word of God. They hold private prayer meetings and worship services. There is a chance they will be beheaded or exiled if discovered. Some of us have heard story after story, but we have become dulled to what people experience for the sake of Christ.

These people are modern-day martyrs. We may never face the same situations, but we still must martyr ourselves to ourselves (Philippians 1:2).

Maybe a day will come when your faith will be challenged in such a matter. What will your response be?

Though you may not realize it, your faith is being challenged even this day. It's a subtle challenge. The actions you manifest each day reveal your response to this challenge. Judge yourself, and see what you need to empty yourself of. Remember, the benefits of emptiness far outweigh what you currently perceive as the benefits of being full.

Chapter 9: Knowing Emptiness

Filled with the Spirit

All around us, there is an invisible battle being waged. If we are perceptive, we can observe it in every issue in life. You can even see it when you watch the national news. One example is the conflict in the Middle East. The root of the conflict in the Middle East is the filling of Jerusalem. God's purpose is to place his name there, filling it with his presence (1 Kings 11:36). Likewise, Satan, knowing God's desire, is attempting to hinder the Father's purpose by placing his name in Jerusalem (Matthew 24:15). This has resulted in an intense global conflict.

Similarly, there is a conflict over who will fill your temple. Both God and Satan desire to fill you. Remember the story of the demoniac in Mark 5 who was filled with a legion of demons. Then there was Mary Magdalene, who had seven evil spirits (Luke 8:2). When Satan and his minions filled these individuals, it brought pain and disease. If not for Jesus, death would have come also. There is no in-between. You have the capacity to be filled with the Spirit. The question is, which one will you choose: death or life?

I do not believe that believers can be possessed. However, Satan will settle for a condolence prize, and that is the oppression of your destiny. Satan's oppression is like when Peter attempted to persuade Jesus not to die on the cross (Matthew 16:23). It can also be the daily struggles you face, something as mundane as attempting to read the Word but finding yourself continually distracted. It could also be on a much grander scale, attempting to remove your destiny and the Word from you.

Early one Saturday morning, about 3:00 a.m., I was in prayer and fasting. I had been sick for weeks. The night before, I was reading the Word and fell asleep on the couch in my living room. I do this often, since the couches are so comfortable. However, I woke up to darkness and discomfort—an unnatural darkness. I had a weird feeling, which I was unable to explain as I woke up. Before me was a dark, shadowy figure. I could see through it. I saw

Chapter 9: Knowing Emptiness

its wicked eyes and the shape of a face as it floated in front of me. There was nowhere for me to go. I was on a couch in the corner, surrounded by it. I attempted to move but was frozen; not one of my body parts responded. Suddenly, it reached out its branch-like arm to me and placed it around my neck.

I couldn't believe what was happening to me. I had seen angels before but not demons. It choked me as I lay there paralyzed. I then began to do the only thing I knew how to do. I attempted to say "Jesus" and pray. But that branch-like arm was hindering my vocal cords. In my heart, I said, *Jesus, help me.* Immediately it released me and floated away. I watched it move backward beyond the wall. This event at the time was very frightening. But it gave me a clearer understanding of the spiritual conflict I was in. The next couple of weeks I experienced a lot of sleepless nights, wondering if I would be attacked again. I even had panic attacks.

Though I didn't see the presence of this evil spirit anymore, there was a darkness surrounding me and attempting to penetrate me. I didn't realize it until I began to come out of it. I found myself clinging to the Word. I wondered why God didn't send an angel to help me out. One day, finally, the tide began to turn. I received a CD teaching from Jentzen Franklin on healing. On this CD he spoke of a very similar situation that had happened to him. It was as if I were living his story. In a strange way, it comforted me. I had read books and seen many testimonies of more horrifying attacks than I experienced, but it's different when you have these types of experiences yourself. It took some time, but I now realize that the message on that CD was the Holy Spirit reaching out to me. It was the Holy Spirit who began not only to fill me during that time but also to comfort me. When we are lacking, hurting, or in physical pain, it only increases the Holy Spirit's desire to be with us. If anyone or anything is coming against us, it only motivates the Spirit to fight on our behalf. First Corinthians 3:16–17 reads, "Do you not know that you

Chapter 9: Knowing Emptiness

are God's temple and that God's Spirit dwells in you? If anyone destroys God's temple, God will destroy him. For God's temple is holy, and you are that temple" (NIV).

The Spirit desires to fill you at this moment. He is real and wants to bring great comfort to you. He is just waiting for you to respond. For me, he sent a CD with a testimony, but for you it could be a letter, or it could be this book, or a call from a friend, urging you to allow the Spirit to fill you.

Quality in Emptiness

The most important element about a sacrifice is its quality. If your sacrifice has no quality, it will not fulfill the requirement of emptiness.

While attending Lincoln University in my undergraduate years, I had one teacher who always demanded quality from me. Dr. Beza made sure I gave my best. He would not accept any half-done assignments. For our midterm, we were assigned to create a presentation on discriminated groups in other societies. He gave us a list of different groups. Out of all of them, one caught my attention: the Kurds in the Middle East.

I struggled to complete this assignment, being a novice in scholarly research. Since I was a student worker at the library, you would think this would be an easy task. But it was a struggle to find credible information. In addition, I was lazy. So I just threw something together, hoping he would let me slide. My soon-to-be wife got out of this presentation by going on a mission trip!

Everyone else in the class gave an excellent presentation. Finally, it was time for me to give mine. My presentation was filled with charts, diagrams, and other documentation. However, most of the numbers and documentation were made up.

Dr. Beza quickly recognized my trickery. He went on to probe me, something he had not done with the others. One question he asked was, "What are the Kurds, and what is their problem?"

I went on to explain that they were a gang in the Middle

Chapter 9: Knowing Emptiness

East and began to use my diagram to explain their territory. Everything began to crumble quickly. My classmates began to laugh as Dr. Beza rendered my presentation void with one question. It was unacceptable. Fortunately for me, he gave me three more chances to present. I finally got it right the fourth time. Occasionally I run into a few of my classmates from this course, and they refer to me as "Kurd."

For me to create an acceptable presentation, I had to give more than time. I had to search online databases for credible information that pertained to my presentation. It stretched my brain in ways I never imagined. This presentation emptied me. In the same way, if our desire is to please God, we must empty ourselves to produce something of quality.

Emptying ourselves often involves a form of humbling ourselves. One way we are to humble ourselves is in worship and adoration to God.

I have been a member of several denominations, and each worshiped God in its own way. In one fellowship, the children pranced around the sanctuary, up and down the aisles, holding hands. Then some of the older members moved gracefully like ballet dancers on the side. Still others simply opened their hymnals and sang praises. One of my favorite hymns is "Holy, Holy, Holy"—this song just gives me goose bumps. There are also those who *shout*. This is when someone is so overcome by the Spirit of God that they jump up and down, run around the sanctuary, or just scream at the top of their lungs. I have also seen others who were so overcome by the Spirit that they fell to their knees before the presence of God.

All of these are forms of worship, but only the Father can discern if one has emptied oneself. The Father is the judge of what is acceptable.

The First Worship Service

In the first recorded worship service on earth, we see both an acceptable and an unacceptable form of worship

Chapter 9: Knowing Emptiness

(Genesis 4). Both Cain and Abel presented God with a gift. However, God only accepted Abel's. What distinguished the gifts is not revealed in Scripture until the New Testament. The writer of Hebrews says Abel offered a more excellent sacrifice (Hebrews 11:4). What made his sacrifice more excellent? Abel emptied himself in his sacrifice.

This is something that cannot be placed on a physical scale to be measured. Only the Spirit of God is able to discern it. As Jesus told the woman at the well, those who worship God must worship in spirit and truth (John 4:24). Often, we judge others' actions based on their outward expressions, but our judgment is frequently wrong. Only those who are able to empty themselves know how to please God. It is hard for those who are rich in self to become empty.

In Matthew 19, we read of a man who followed all the commandments, and Jesus asked him to sell all he owned and give to the poor. But this man was unwilling to make this sacrifice; it was too much for him. He was unable to empty himself of finances.

What about you? It might not be money that prevents you from giving your all to God. It could be a degree, your reputation, your family, or the traditions of men. Don't let these finite things prevent the infinite from being accomplished in your life. When you empty yourself, you realize there is nothing within yourself that can accomplish what God has ordained for you to do. Empty, you are ready to receive all you need from him.

The End of the Beginning

The plot is composed of five elements. Those elements are the exposition, rising action, climax, falling action, and the resolution. Our lives often mirror a Hollywood movie storyline. As a matter of fact, real life inspires many of those movies! Each of us can relate to experiencing conflict, climax, and the seemingly mundane exposition. But how many of us have experienced the resolution?

Chapter 9: Knowing Emptiness

Very few have.

Others have occasionally found some glimmer of it, only to discover a new conflict or the same conflict awaiting them around the corner. So where is our resolution?

My journey with God has taken me places I never imagined I would go. I began it on paved roads with signs and markings. These markings helped keep me on track. As my journey progressed, the paved roads turned into gravel roads. Gravel roads turned into muddy paths. Muddy paths led me to what seemed like an endless forest to nowhere. I journeyed so deep in the forest that the trees blocked my view of the sun. Even rays of light were unable to penetrate this place. Occasionally my journey led me to places I had been before. I would often come across an abandoned house. There was nothing special or unusual about this place. The windows were cracked. Portions of the outside looked as if they had been burnt. Grass was growing through the crevasses of the front porch. There were holes in the roof. The yard was a forest. It had not seen a lawnmower in years. Its appearance was uninviting. But one day, I was drawn to this abandoned house as if it were beckoning me to enter. The door was sealed from the outside with a four-by-four. A sign hung on it that said, NO TRESPASSING. But surely no one remembered this place! It was forsaken and forgotten. No one would care if I entered.

The barricade of lumber was easy to pry off as I opened the door. Inside, it was like every other abandoned house. I went from room to room as I entered deeper into the house, drawn in like a fish on a hook. With each step I took, the ground creaked in pain as if it begged for restoration. I wondered, could this house speak?

With that question, it was as if a faint voice began to grow stronger. In this empty place I began to feel a sense of familiarity, as if I were the one who owned this decayed place. Suddenly, gusts of wind whisked down the hallway. Their force slammed the door that was only a few feet in front of me shut.

Chapter 9: Knowing Emptiness

I began to think about all of the scary movies I had seen over the years. Anytime you have doors closing and voices telling you to get out, that should be a sign to leave! But I wasn't deterred. I continued my investigation. If death was behind that door, I was dying today. After all, I had no other place to look. Plus, I didn't hear an audible voice that said, "Get out," even though there was an unmistakable presence inside of that house urging me to leave. Yet, there was another sensation pressing me to go further.

I tried to open the door that had slammed shut. It was much more difficult to open than the front door, as if someone was pushing from the other side. This only made me more determined. When I finally pried opened the door, I saw something I wasn't expecting. In the middle of the floor was an old treasure chest. From the chest, illuminating rays penetrated the slight opening. As I opened it, I felt as if my journey was complete—but also just beginning. I had found what I was searching for in the least-expected place. What I found was an unlimited treasure. My resolution!

I'm still trying to count my spoils today. But what is important about the story is my connection to the forsaken house. The building was a representation of me. Perhaps it also represents you. Do you feel forsaken? Abandoned or forgotten? Is your life comparable to this abandoned place? Many of us search and search for our resolution. But we often neglect to look in the one place where we will find the answer. We search the airwaves, our best friend, and fortune cookies, but we neglect to look within. We see ourselves as nothing more than an abandoned building, a good-for-nothing. Yet our heavenly Father has placed a treasure within us (2 Peter 1:3). This treasure causes us to be more than conquerors, and it will lead you to your destiny.

Perhaps now is a good time to end this discussion. I have taken you as far as I can toward your destiny. I know I have been vague by not giving more specific directions. You may have the feeling that I have led you to a dead

Chapter 9: Knowing Emptiness

end, that I have not given you what you need. But I have not been given the power to give you what you need. God reserves that for himself. It is comparable to when you want to give a gift to someone special. You don't want to send it via mail, nor would you desire to have someone else give it. You want to give it to them personally. You want to see the joy on their face.

This is God's desire. God wants to give you his mysteries face-to-face. My hope in writing this book was just to start you on the journey. So there is no need to worry; the Holy Spirit will lead you further. We must think of ourselves as pilgrims. Many pilgrims left everything they knew for the uncertain. They left routine and rituals behind for the New World.

If we want our destiny to manifest, we must also voyage to the uncertain. Yet, on this voyage, we need search no further than within ourselves (John 18:23). There, we will not find ourselves but what God has placed within us. We must not think that we have all knowledge and power, for we are nothing without him. Your hope is Jesus, but he is in you.

A man lived on this earth not that long ago who was intrigued by the peanut. He often wondered why God would make such a thing. For days, this man *locked* himself in his laboratory with nothing but a peanut, his equipment, and the Word of God. He asked God to unlock the mysteries of the peanut. God revealed to him over three hundred uses for the peanut. Among them were cosmetics, dyes, printer ink, paints, plastics, shaving cream, and gasoline. He said, "Only alone can I draw close enough to God to discover His secrets." This man was the inventor George Washington Carver. He spoke of having intimate talks with God in his laboratory, which he referred to as "God's Little Workshop." We too must be like Carver and lock ourselves up with God so he can unlock the mysteries he desires to show us. Wherever you find to be alone with him is your "secret place," as unique as your thumbprint. God will speak to each of us in our own "Little Workshop."

Chapter 9: Knowing Emptiness

I believe that in each one of us before the foundation of the earth was established, God placed a destiny. For each of us it is something different. You may hold the key to the automobile that runs on water. Perhaps the gift of healing is lying dormant within you. You will never know unless you develop your own secret place.

Don't believe that you are insignificant in the plan of God. You were destined for this generation, for a time like today. Now, like our slave friends who pursued freedom, the choice is yours. The Holy Spirit has used me as a vessel to reveal the concealed to you. But you have to take the journey. And you can only begin your journey by becoming empty.

I pray that we will empty ourselves of traditions and beliefs contrary to God's plan for his kingdom. My hope is that once we have emptied ourselves and become hungry for God, our desire for God will increase. That our food will become to do the will of God, like it was for Jesus (John 4:34). God has placed the ball in your hands. He is more than just a coach giving you directions from the sideline.

He is placing wisdom within you, wisdom that your enemy cannot comprehend.

God's wisdom is unlimited, just like his house. In John 14:2, Jesus says, "In my father's house are many mansions" (NIV). How can one house hold one mansion, let alone many? You can spend a lot of time thinking about this statement, or you can use that time to experience it. Just like wisdom: we can think about how wonderful it is, or we can apply it. This is a choice we face with every tick of the clock.

From the ancient times, your destiny was ordained by God. This destiny purses and desires to overtake you. But you must choose it in return. Jeremiah 6:16 reads, "This is what the LORD says: 'Stand at the crossroads and look; ask for the ancient paths, ask where the good way is, and walk in it, and you will find rest for your souls.' But you said, 'We will not walk in it.'" Even at this moment,

Chapter 9: Knowing Emptiness

you're at a crossroad. God is saying, "Ask me to show you the ancient path, the good way, the way of destiny." Your destiny is to be the bride of Christ without spot, wrinkle, or blemish (Ephesians 5:22 NIV). This is not something you become when Christ returns but something you are now. You are holy and blameless in his sight. This is the key to manifesting your destiny.

This is the ancient path you must choose. Becoming the bride of Christ is not simply a onetime choice. It's a daily choice. Each day, through your actions, you either choose to be a bride without spot or wrinkle or you choose not to be. Let's not make the mistake of waiting for the rapture to come because then everything will be okay.

This attitude will cause you to forsake manifesting your destiny as the bride of Christ. I too once stood in that place. I was waiting for the rapture because I knew when that happened, everything would be okay. But my waiting has changed. I do not wait for God to come.

Instead, I realize he is already here, waiting to be manifested through us. He is waiting for us to move in authority and power. In Isaiah 45:11, God says, "Thus saith the LORD, the Holy One of Israel, and his Maker, Ask me of things to come concerning my sons, and concerning the work of my hands command ye me" (KJV). Our destiny will not simply come to us. We choose it. Your picking this book up was not by chance. It was a way of you asking God to show you the ancient path, the God way. Now God has shown you how to begin your journey toward destiny. But will you take it? Will you walk down this path? If you do not choose the ancient path, you will forfeit manifesting your destiny. Let's not bypass destiny but make today a day of destiny.

This choice of manifesting your destiny is not only for your own sake. The ultimate purpose of manifesting your destiny is for all of creation. Just for a moment, think of those struggling. It could be a neighbor, friend, cousin, or mother. They could be saved or unsaved. You must manifest your destiny for them.

Chapter 9: Knowing Emptiness

The pastors of my church told me of a dream they'd had. In their dream, scores of people were attempting to enter an already full sanctuary.

All of these people were searching for something—something they couldn't find outside of the presence of God. God has chosen to use us as a vessel, a pipeline to manifest his glory, purpose, and destiny. There is a hope within you. Only you can bring it out. The minister on television can't, and neither can the evangelist coming into town for revival. They can lead you to the front door, but you have to enter destiny. Many—so many—are waiting on you. What's at stake is more than you can comprehend! The bird that flies from north to south, the ocean waves that are set in motion by the moon, and galaxies that no man can number or telescope has observed are waiting on you.

About the Author

I am what I am, a person with great expectations and hope. Just like you, I'm just passing through this world, trying to make a difference. At a mere glance, I'm just an ordinary person. I don't claim to know all, and neither have I experienced it all. I only hope to help and be a true friend on your journey. If you're looking for a perfect, know-it-all, person, you're looking in the wrong direction. My mistakes are too many to number. You may have even noticed some in this book. I am no better than you. Yet l strive to be perfect and manifest unlimited wisdom. My hope is to reflect wisdom and perfect that which resides within me through Christ so you and I may know the Father in a personal way. Some of the organizations I'm a part of include Toastmasters, Heart of America Christian Writers' Network (HACWN), Inspire Christian Writers, International Fellowship of Christian Ministers (IFCM), Order of St. Luke's Ministry, House of Refuge of Jefferson City, Missouri (Pastor Alfonse and Jennifer Webb), Equipping the Believers, a Ministry of Jubilee Ministry of Olathe, Kansas (Pastor Dan Crevier), and Jesus Christ Ministries (Pastor James Vivian).

To find out more about Jamere, visit www.jamere.org.

Salvation Prayer
Have you ever made Jesus the Lord and Savior of your life?
If not, pray this prayer and start a new life in Christ.

Dear God,
I come to You in the Name of Jesus. I admit that I am not right with You, and I want to be right with You. I ask You to forgive me of all my sins. The Bible says if I confess with my mouth that "Jesus is Lord," and believe in my heart that God raised Him from the dead, I will be saved (Rom. 10:9). I believe with my heart and I confess with my mouth that Jesus is the Lord and Savior of my life. Thank You for saving me!
In Jesus' Name l pray. Amen.